REALITY AND MYTH
When Two Worlds Collide

Gabriel Delvis Roy

INDIA • SINGAPORE • MALAYSIA

Notion Press

Old No. 38, New No. 6
McNichols Road, Chetpet
Chennai - 600 031

First Published by Notion Press 2018
Copyright © Gabriel Delvis Roy 2018
All Rights Reserved.

ISBN
Hardcase 978-1-64249-868-4
Paperback 978-1-64249-839-4

This book has been published with all reasonable efforts taken to make the material error-free after the consent of the author. No part of this book shall be used, reproduced in any manner whatsoever without written permission from the author, except in the case of brief quotations embodied in critical articles and reviews.

The Author of this book is solely responsible and liable for its content including but not limited to the views, representations, descriptions, statements, information, opinions and references ["Content"]. The Content of this book shall not constitute or be construed or deemed to reflect the opinion or expression of the Publisher or Editor. Neither the Publisher nor Editor endorse or approve the Content of this book or guarantee the reliability, accuracy or completeness of the Content published herein and do not make any representations or warranties of any kind, express or implied, including but not limited to the implied warranties of merchantability, fitness for a particular purpose. The Publisher and Editor shall not be liable whatsoever for any errors, omissions, whether such errors or omissions result from negligence, accident, or any other cause or claims for loss or damages of any kind, including without limitation, indirect or consequential loss or damage arising out of use, inability to use, or about the reliability, accuracy or sufficiency of the information contained in this book.

Dedicated to my loving wife
Vimala Johncibel Roy

Contents

Foreword — *xiii*
Preface — *xxi*
Acknowledgements — *xxvii*

Section 1: Waiting

Lonely Without You…	3
In My Sight…	5
To the Temple…	7
Untitled 1…	8
Do You Know…	10
Memories…	12
Yesterday Is Gone…	14
Waiting for You, My Beloved…	16
Two Worlds Collide…	18
Warm Within…	19
Being You…	20
Waiting to Hear Your Voice…	22
Failed to Express…	23
Missing You…	24
In Your Arms…	25
Do You Know…	26
Words with No Meaning…	27

Is It Real or a Dream…	29
A Long Time…	31
My Heart Says…	32
This Waiting…	34
At Arms' Reach…	36
New Meaning…	37
Magic of Love…	38
Longing…	39
Remember When…	41
I Need You…	42
Be Near to Me…	43
Say I Love You…	44

Section 2: Dreams

Memories and Dreams…	47
It's Fairies' Time…	49
Really…	51
Dancing Like a Pretty Queen…	52
Are They Only Dreams…	53
First Distant Sight…	55
One with Me…	56
End My Dreams…	58
These Are My Dreams…	59
Do You Know My Dreams…	61
The Music and Your Fragrance…	62
Dreams…	64
Words Made No Meaning…	65
Hey, What Are You Thinking…	66

Section 3: Friends

If I Could Share His Song…	69
Precious Moments…	71

My First Friend…	72
Since I Said Good Bye…	74
How Can I Forget…	75
My Love It's You….	78
Friendship…	80
Is It Real…	81
As You Travel…	84
Friends…	85
How Can I Forget – The Tsunami…	87
Going Away…	90
Days In Nagoya…	91
Dear Beverly…	92
When I Was Young…	94
To Rosy…	96
To You Kazimierz…	100
As I Recall…	102
To a Good Friend…	104
Dear Ms. Kathy Tyson…	106
Gone to the Yonder…	107
Few Words of Farewell…	108
Out of Control…	110
Oh! Flint How Much You Suffer…	111
Born to Paint…	114
To Sasha My Friend…	116

Section 4: Thoughts

It's a Miracle…	121
Without You…	123
Memories, Sweet Memories…	124
A Fairy Princess…	125
I Think of Thee…	127

The Old Cuff Links…	129
Lost In Thoughts…	131
Thoughts…	133
Need You Now…	135
Whispering Wind…	137
Happy Birthday…	139
Random Thoughts and Unanswered Questions…	141
If I Could Read My Mind…	144
Where Are the Words…	146
It Must Be You…	148
Untitled 2…	150
A Star to Catch…	152
Irony of Love…	153
Still Thinking of You…	157
Someday Soon…	158
Watching You…	159
My Friend…	160

Section 5: Family

Abandoned…	165
Thinking of You Mom…	168
Dreamed of a Girl…	171
God's Own Country…	173
My Little Girl…	175
Awaiting Surgery…	177
Her World…	178
Back Home Again…	180
Christmas from Far Away…	183
Still New…	185
Memories and Hope…	186
New Year…	188

My Valentine…	190
How I Feel…	192
Thinking About My Home…	195
My Mother…	197
Unknown Search…	199
So Much to Say…	200
Sick and Lonesome…	202
To You Mother, From Miles Away…	203
Shattered Dreams…	205
Remembering My Valentine…	209
My Father…	211
Just a While…	213
His Mercy Never Fails…	214
How Fragile I Am…	217

Section 6: Love

Do You Remember the Day…	221
Two Worlds…	223
Above All…	225
Want to Write…	226
Love…	227
I Asked…	229
God's Love…	231
Mystery Still Unfolded…	233
What About Love…	234
You Asked Me…	236
It's So Hard to Say Good-Bye…	237
You Are…	239
On Love…	244
Then…	246
You Are, to Me…	247

Reason to Love…	249
More Aspects of Love…	251
The Greatest Gift…	254
Giving and Sharing…	255
A Corner In My Heart…	257
Why Didn't I…	258
Life's Blessed Moments…	260
See In Me…	262
A World of Reality and Myth…	263
Belonging to Each Other…	265
Need Love…	266
This World's Pressures…	268
Lost World…	269
From Within…	271

Section 7: Passion

Lingers In My Mind…	275
Follow You…	277
This Night…	279
Rapture of the Cherry Blossom…	282
Different Expressions…	284
To Be With You…	286
Enduring Love…	287
Path to Passion…	289
Lost In Your Love…	291
Though Faraway…	293
Those Were the Years…	295
On Your Lap, Like a Babe…	297
Lost In You…	299

Section 8: Pain

The Song I Never Wrote…	303
Do You Know How Much…	305
Longing for Happiness…	307
Lost In Your Thoughts…	309
That Old Picture…	312
Confused…	313
Feeling Like a Clown…	315
If the Word 'Sorry' Makes Any Sense…	316
Looking for Words…	317
Withering Away…	318
Tossed Between Reality and Myth…	319
If Only I Could Have Saved That Life…	321
Freedom In Bondage…	323
The Dark Side…	325
Is It Love…	326
Is the Soul Forgotten…	328
Troubled Times…	329
There Was a Time…	332
Tarnished Pages…	333
Difficult Times…	334
Calm After Storm…	335
What Have I Done…	337
Can You Tell Me…	338
If You Ask Me…	339
Seems Like Yesterday…	340

Section 9: Hope

True Peace…	345
Wounded Bird…	347

Sharing Your Pain…	348
War for No Reason…	350
Out of Control…	351
Willing, but Forbidden…	352
The Burning Candle…	353
Need Someone…	355
Real Freedom…	357
Don't Be Blue…	358
Easing My Pain…	360
Hard Times…	362
Will You Forgive Me…	363
Those Memories…	365
You Are the One…	367
Her Prayer Will Be Heard…	369
A Little Rose Bud…	370
In My Heart…	371
Wearied Moments…	373
Turbulent Waters…	374
I'll Make It Up With You…	375
You Are…	376
Are You Drifting Away…	377
Beyond Words…	378
Life's Precious Moments…	379
Rays of Hope…	380

Illustrations are by the author

Foreword

Mind is the seat of poetry and heart is its soul. So goes the poetic dictum of one of the greatest trio of Tamil literary Renaissance at the onset of the twentieth century, Kavimoni, a son of the native soil, that has also given birth to yet another poet, perhaps not writing in Tamil, his birth-language, but in English, an acquired but later naturalized literary creative idiom, Gabriel Delvis Roy (Roy for short), an indigenous counterpart of Kavimoni.

But then, to Kavimoni, poetry is the finest human expression couched in the artless, yet the most exalted artistic language or literary expression as it were, that would profoundly unfold the truth and reveal the underlying quest of the human heart in all its passionate intensity for liberation, consolation and poetic relief. And poetry offers the rapturous joy of pure ecstasy that it shall always remain both for the maker and the reader cathartic and liberative. And what a striking coincidence between the two gentle, sober and spontaneously emotional poetic output of Kavimoni and Roy – a coincidence that is not accidental, nor co-incidental at all, but is undoubtedly providential indeed.

It is true that the poetic canvas of Roy is certainly not as vast and as rigorous as in Kavimoni; but the depth of experience that goes into the making of the very fibre of his poetic output synchronizes, to a stunning extent with that of Kavimoni in every domain of creativity. And a student of literature, maybe in the days to come, would do well to attempt a comparative study of the major themes dealt with by both the poets, except those that deal with the themes of love and longing, separation and seclusion. And Kavimoni and Roy are gifts of this God's land, the southern-most tip of India, to the traditionally ancient Tamil literary heritage and the new but evocatively enterprising Indo-Anglian literature or Indian Writing in English.

Roy's first poetic collection (his maiden attempt at publishing poetry) is a welcome addition for the simple reason that, even a cursory reading of the poems included in *Reality and Myth* speaks volumes about the poetic potential of a searching heart that aesthetically looks for an emotional outlet through 'the wings of poesy', unmistakably shows a serious poet in the making in Roy. The temporal spectrum of the poetic sparks, that find their berth in Roy's maiden compilation, is at once long and large enough, spanning over a fairly impressive period of his poetic career ranging from a care-free youth to a serious scholar, culminating with the 'mindset' of a meta-physicist that philosophically mellows down with the passing of age and thus becomes ripe enough to view life with a greater degree of disinterestedness and dispassionate detachment. And that provides the legitimate critical space to gauge and evaluate the evolution of the poetic mind, in all its gay and gladness, passing through an unbearable cauldron of agony and a 'feel of rootlessness' at its peak, and landing in the God-given space of tranquility and reconciliation, the inevitable part of life that one comes to grip with, which precisely offers itself as the poetic truth, in the final analysis of one's life. But one has to necessarily pass through the chamber of, to borrow a phrase form that immortal Romantic poet, John Keats, the happiness of the mind, the heaviness of the heart and ultimately the healing of the soul.

Roy's *Reality and Myth* traverses through the poetic path, beginning with Waiting, through Dreams, Friends, Thoughts, Family, Love, Passion, Pain and culminating in, obviously, Hope, hopefully radiating with an affirmation of life that despite and in the midst of hardship, misfortune, disasters and loss that ravage the human life, life is still worth living with faith and hope.

Like the Elizabethan Wyatt and Surrey, here is a poetic mind soaked in love, longing for the loved ones, evidently in a surreal world, that literally transports the readers to a world of his own imagination, at times bordering on juvenile love and craving for lasting relationship. The poet is a worshipper of the beauty of love, like the Pre-Raphaelites, just for the sake of beauty and love. And this gives him the added strength to venerating the ecstasy of love, just for the sake of heart's fulfillment, and when transcended spiritual fulfillment. A few snippets culled out from a few pages would clearly demonstrate, besides the artistic expositions of the subject matter the poet chose for himself, the rhythmic, mellifluous flow of his poetry, a refreshing cadence surged with an inundated, powerful overflow of spontaneous expressions that lend a poetic charm to the variegated tapestry of the solid poetic structure.

> Come to me, my symphony,
> I'm waiting for that harmony.
> If waiting can make one rich and wiser,
> How rich and wiser I will be this winter! (34)

> Breath mixes with breath creating a legacy,
> Bodies radiate creating an eternal ecstasy,
> And minds are entwined as a divine symphony;
> Memories and dreams, Oh! What a perfect harmony! (48)

> I could never forget Ram for a long time, he was right in
>   front of me

That lean, short man in torn clothes, and the words he
 spoke to me;
But it's his kindness and his care for others that touched my heart!
I spoke of him in several meetings as the most important person I
 ever met
In my life – which I said with pride and truthfulness from within.
It has been more than forty years since I met him on that
 unforgettable morn,
I could not see him again as I told him then, not sure if he is in this
 world,
But as I type this, tears from my eyes prevent me from seeing the
 keyboard. (77)

I think of the vanity of human wishes and the paths to achieve
 those,
I think of the hatred and jealousy that have taken over mankind;
The unwanted wars and killings, that make no sense, make me
 shiver.
I wish and pray that a day may come that everyone realizes
That we are all part of a large family, rich and poor, black and white
But all tied with a supreme bond – the bond of being a
 human. (89)

It seems some portion of our society had lost its sanity,
A crying child's voice out of pain is seldom respected or heard;
Those in power want more power and seek after vanity,
And the mother's plea for a dying child is often ignored.
Do these hypocrites think that their blood is thicker than the rest,
That the poor can be easily bought and sold – it's just insanity,
They will have to answer to the one above us one day at last,

But, we have to act as human beings and are here to save
    humanity. (113)

There is a song, still unwritten, in my heart,
The song I'll sing for you, when you come back to me,
There is one tune for my guitar, I have never played
And I'll play it for you, when you sing with me; (124)

If I have only one life
I wish that life is for loving! (151)

Overlooking the mighty LA harbor
Her body sleeps in the deep shelter
And when I place a bouquet beside her
I hear her say, "Daddy please don't cry!" (176)

Even after I am gone, I'll still be with you, can't leave you,
Close your eyes and ears, you will hear me whispering to you;
I will be around you to see you happy and to protect you
And my soul will wish many many happy birthdays to you. (201)

If memories held dear can become real again
And if I have wings to carry me back again
To the times that so swiftly passed away,
How happy I could be in every way! (303)

I still long for a journey in this world
With understanding and resolve so bold
That true happiness will be on my way
Beyond the words I have learned can say. (378)

Foreword

Was it C. Day Lewis who once said that a creative mind finds its 'credibility' in the curious collocation of words and phrases, a mysterious combination which is refreshingly new and unanticipated, and thus it enhances the linguistic possibility of exploiting the language to yield fragrant idioms and figures of speech which is, after all, the touchstone of creativity. Here are a few of the poet's collocations that are the eternal joy of the metaphor and oxymoron, metonymy and synecdoche and more than that 'new additions' to and 'new arrivals' in English

> voice brushes the ear (10)
> spoken words are hard to find (11)
> lovely ear blush (16)
> thought of my lips (16)
> with fragrance from the autumn wind (20)
> melody with a new touch (25)

True that the themes overlap sometimes the subject matters are repetitive, but that which concretizes every poetic creation of Roy is the uniqueness of the message and the transcendent contextualization of the poetic experience which lends a subtle individuality to every poem, that it stands all by itself, as an autonomous slice of life. And this is precisely what one finds even in the writings of quite a few of the 'greats' and the 'great of the greats.'

Kanniyakumari District can richly boast of its English education, thanks to the sacrificial efforts of the equally sacrificial missionaries of the erstwhile London Missionary Society (LMS), who for the first time founded Western-model English schools (William Tobias Ringeltaube [1809], Charles Mead [1819], Johanna Celestina Mead and Martha Mault [1819], James Duthie [1893]) that historically opened up vistas of channels of knowledge acquisition and proficiency in English by all communities, most of which until then were deprived, and deliberately denied of the fruits of learning and scholarship purely on extraneous considerations of caste and colour. And the pent-up product was explosively productive. And thus we have had a fairly representative and long line of English poets, M.D. Daniel, perhaps the first Indian English Writer (poet) in South Travancore, followed by the legendary Hepziba Jesudasan, V. Sam Sahayam (published by P. Lal's Writers' Workshop, Kolkata), and Mycia Daniel. And *Reality and Myth*, certainly not an exaggeration to say that, has catapulted, and quite judiciously at that, Gabriel Delvis Roy, into the ever shining pantheon of eternal artists and poets from this tiny district, who by sheer dint of the intrinsic value of their literary creativity have earned for themselves a permanence that will linger on in the ages and ages to come. Let me congratulate the poet Roy on his very successful maiden poetic venture. And may he beget many more such buxom poetic off-springs, hale, healthy and remarkably impressive indeed.

E. James R. Daniel,
President, Association of Global South Studies
South Asia Chapter (AGSS – SAC)
Hon. Director, Chair on Christian Studies,
Manonmaniam Sundaranar University, Thirunelveli and
Formerly Principal, Scott Christian College (Autonomous, Nagercoil)

Preface

While I retire to my bed to invite sleep that will dissolve the day's toils and worries, sometimes I am lost in the memories past – memories of the old and new – memories of unforgettable days and thoughts about the fragments of painful pleasure that are to be forgotten, but still linger in my mind. Some leave a feeling of accomplishment, while the other leave only memories, short, but strong enough to penetrate through the periphery of my heart. I cannot forget the time I spent with my friends. Sharing their joy and sorrow have made permanent impressions in my mind. It will be very satisfying to share all these with you my readers. Before I give an introduction to this book of poems, I would like to introduce me to you.

I am Gabriel Delvis Roy, known as Gabriel to my friends and colleagues in the U.S. and other countries, as Delvis to my friends, classmates and colleagues in India, and simply as Roy to my family folks. From my younger years, there are two things I loved and still love most – painting and writing, and obviously wanted to be a painter or a writer or both! As I remember, I could draw an elephant, or a dog better than I could write the letters of the alphabet, when I was four. My father was a good artist, and everybody attributed my aptitude for painting to my father. He showed me how to mix the basic colors to make the color of our choice, how to make a frame and attach the canvas to it and even how to frame the paintings! I did not get the opportunity to see my

Preface

father paint because he was too busy as a head master and assisting in managing three schools for the parish. Being the only grandchild in the joint family home for a few years, I got all the attention from my dear ones, and from my uncle who was a true scholar in English.

Before I even got to the preparatory class – the current fifth grade – he made me familiar with the legends like Shakespeare, Wordsworth, Ruskin, Tolstoy and many more and their works. I finished my high school when I was thirteen and could not get admission to college being too young. I was so disappointed that I had to stay home for a year when my friends took off to colleges. But I am thankful for that, as it gave me the opportunity to study painting for a year.

When I asked my father that I want to go to Mumbai (Bombay in those years) to study painting and to be a professional artist or to study English literature in Thiruvananthapuram, he did not accept it. He made it very clear that I must study Engineering or Medicine and that I can always paint or write as a hobby. I truly appreciate his decision because science and engineering have always been good to me in my life. I have my dreams about painting accomplished by exhibiting my paintings in Art Festivals, having one-man shows, winning awards, and even making money selling my paintings during my college years! I have included a few of my old and new paintings in this book.

Though I contributed poems and articles to magazines and other publications, the poems I wrote over the years, since I was fourteen were packed and stored in shoe boxes or later in file folders. To me poetry is a form of communication in very simple language, adding some rhyme to the lines, expressing what I felt with truthfulness, and the reader can feel what I felt. Some of the poems, I have included in this book were written on paper napkins while I was having coffee or dinner in a restaurant, on airplane boarding cards or on hotel note pads. I used to draw pictures of professors during their class lectures or write poems about the thoughts that would have gone through the minds of those who wrote the books that we were studying. Crazy, it may sound, but I enjoyed it.

One event comes to my mind. It was English poetry class in college. My professor was teaching Shakespeare's Midsummer Night's Dream. In the class test he asked us to 'draw the character sketch of the clown whom you like most from this story.' I drew a picture in pencil of Nick Bottom and queen Titania embracing him. He gave me zero out of ten for the test. But I told him that I deserve more because I have given him my sincere answer.

"I wanted an essay, not a drawing," said the professor.
"But you have asked to draw a sketch, and that's what I did!"
"You have a point there, bring your sketch back."
I gave my drawing back to him, He added a one to the left of the zero. I said,
"Thank you so much sir!" and got back the drawing.
"Give it back to me."
He got the drawing back and added a minus one to it, saying,
"Remember, even a rose flower in a paddy field is weed, and it should be plucked off!"

I could never forget that day and that conversation with my (late) Prof. T. Y. Harris.

This book is a collection of poems written over five decades. My friends have been encouraging me over the years to put the poems written at random in a book form. They were written during my college years, during my career as a professor in engineering college and as a research manager during conferences and meetings, and a few very recently – up to last week. So, you will find poems relating to those who are young in heart and those who are old, but still are young in heart! I have added a couple of my paintings done in the Nineteen Seventies and last month!

Before I started to collect poems for this, my first book in literature, from the pile of poems written over the years on very different subjects, I closed my eyes and sat quiet on my chair before my computer. In the endless ocean of my thoughts, I asked my mind, "How can I swim across the deep waters and reach the unreachable shores to find eternal happiness?" Then I heard my master saying, "You don't have to go that far for happiness and peace of mind. It's here close to you. If you can give happiness to someone for a moment, count that as eternal happiness to you!" And I said, "Master, when I try to give happiness to those I love, I give them pain without my knowing. How can one find happiness in pain?" And the master said, "It is not your fault my son, my people have tried to put barriers to love. And they know not they are putting themselves into prisons from which they cannot escape. Let not your love be masked by the gloom of mankind. Love the one who loves you, love has no barrier, and love never ends." I said, "Master, I will, no matter what comes on the way."

Then I was walking in darkness, depressed, not knowing where I was going, nor who will help me. Suddenly, a lightning came, and I found the way. And I heard my master saying, "Son, just as you know not where the lightning came from and where it has gone, people unknown to you will help you when you are in need, will love you when you are abandoned. For what on earth is more blessed than helping and loving one another!"

It was like waking up from a dream – rather from a vision. So, I decided that the theme of this book is going to be love and the aspects related to love. I wrote a poem on the story of my birth, and it is included as "Abandoned…" in this book. That is the first experience of love shown by a stranger to me, the love of a nurse shown towards a child on the day he was born!

The book is divided in to nine sections: 1. Waiting, 2. Dreams, 3. Friends, 4. Thoughts, 5. Family, 6. Love, 7. Passion, 8. Pain and 9. Hope. Though in Section 3 (Friends) and Section 5 (Family), I write about the realities of love and pain, challenges and God's guidance, I encountered, the overall theme of the book is about different shades of love. The remaining poems, although divided among seven sections, are truly about the longing, the affirmation, the disappointments, and final overcoming of these human feelings in ways that are different for different individuals. You will see these emotions intertwined in the poems as well.

A very young man was sitting near a beach playing a sad melody with his guitar. It really touched my heart and I wrote, 'If only I could share his song.' The tragedy that took place in Flint or the aftermath of the Tsunami prompted me to put my feeling in simple words to share with others. The remarkable life of ordinary folks around me, their influence in my own life and the pain of their loss are reflected in the poems, 'To Rosy' and 'To Sasha my friend.'

Imagination is like a bird that flies free where ever it wants to so long as there is wind below its wings. So was my situation. I was so busy with the pursuit of science, yet met several people during my endless journey, far and near, who have provided inspiration to rekindle my imagination and passion for writing. It's fairy's time, Rapture of the cherry blossom, Days in Nagoya, A world of reality and myth – all depict the thoughts that went through my mind when I was at different places.

Preface

Though I have been writing poems over several years, now only I got the opportunity to publish them in a book form. I have picked, for this book, the poems depicting an overall theme of love and its many colors, the associated longing, waiting, rapture, agony, pain and hope. Again, I want to let my readers know that these poems are either spontaneous or immersed feelings of my heart or imagination transformed into words. I do hope that you will enjoy reading this, and perhaps shed a tear drop or two trickling down your cheeks.

Connect with the author:
Gabriel D. Roy
Email: roygd@aol.com
Mobile phone: +1 571-418-9333

Acknowledgements

Though my friends and colleagues insisted that I continue to do what I was doing, I thought it is time to get away from that pursuit and spend my time to fulfil my dream that was left behind for decades – to compile together and publish my poems. Though the intention was there, the execution part of it wasn't easy. My wife, Vimala has always been an inspiration and she used to remind me everyday to write "something!" But writing that something wasn't also that easy due to the unexpected chores that came by. On occasions like Christmas, New year and other events, my daughters in law Vino and Rita used to read them to all and tell me to publish them. My daughter Sitara, who is working on a Children's book is a critic and her encouragement meant a lot to me. My thanks to them all. Another person from my family to whom I want to express my thanks is not here, but her soul will be listening to this. She is my daughter Suchitra. When she was young, I used to write to her pages and pages of letters, during my travels. "Dad, this is going to be a Discovery of the World, when published, But, keep writing your poems!" she used to say.

I wish to acknowledge a good friend of mine, Prof. Gloria Devaraj for her constant reminders to publish the book, and her valuable suggestions. I am delighted to acknowledge Prof. James R. Daniel, President, Association of Global Studies, South Asia Chapter, Former Head of the Department of English and Principal of Scott Christian College,

Acknowledgements

Nagercoil, for writing the Foreword to this book, and also for his words of appreciation and encouragement. There are so many friends, who come to my mind, for encouraging me and sometimes insisting to write poems during meetings and conferences, reading them and often translating them into other languages. My sincere thanks to all those who inspired me during difficult times to keep on writing. I wrote the Foreword to a book written by my nephew Gordon and published by Notion Press. I thank him for introducing me to Notion Press during this visit to India. I had the opportunity to meet the staff at Notion Press and I appreciate the interest they have shown and publishing this book. In particular, I express my sincere thanks and appreciation to Ms. Charmine Joseph for her meticulous care and attention to detail in the publication of the book. It has been a pleasure working with her. I like to thank Mr. Praveen Raj and Ms. Shiny Grace, also of Notion Press for their assistance.

For everything there is a time, and so for publishing this book. I thank God for making this happen.

Section 1

Waiting

Buds wait to bloom, withered trees wait for the spring to have new leaves, paddy fields wait for the rain – we all wait for something at one time or the other. It may be waiting for the airplane to land or for the holidays. But there are so many events and moments there we wait for. When I close my eyes and try to get some sleep, sometimes my own waiting and those of my friends come before my eyes.

Lonely Without You...

It is late at night, I could hardly sleep;
    I touched my side, you were not there!
Memories that you left for me to keep
    Are the only comfort and solace here!

The Eiffel tower stood tall and bright
    Amidst the hot and humid summer air,
Sound of music filled the sultry night
    But the loneliness without you, I can't bear.

Come to me sweetheart, at least in my dreams
    And touch me, kiss me, satisfy my desire!
Seems like ages since I had you in my arms,
    Embrace me and fill me with your soothing fire!

I am surrounded by young and old
    Having cell phones in their hands
They talk endlessly, in tones soft and loud,
    Those chain of words love inspires!

Love conquers both young and old,
    Expects nothing at all in return

Except only to be faithfully loved
    With hearts beat in divine union.

Turn your ears to my heart's beat,
    You will hear it spell your name;
Come to me my beloved, I can't wait,
    Give me the warmth of your tender frame.

Only you and you alone can fill my heart,
    Lift it to the heights of endless ecstasy;
Give a new meaning to its every beat
    And fulfill every kind of dream and fantasy!

In My Sight…

I didn't think of you last night,
But still you're in my sight
So vivid and clear
And so very near!
I dare not tell you what we talked about,
All that I can say – it was so sweet
To be with you again
And memories still remain
So strong that they penetrate
Into my heart and recreate
New enchanting visions,
Reaching new horizons!
Mind is a terrible thing that can never forget
Each day I spent with you until you left!

To the Temple…

Like a fairy princess, to the temple, she tiptoed
On that rough and winding narrow gravel road,
As she saw me looking straight at her face
She blushed, her face turned into a beautiful rose.

I couldn't stop taking my eyes away from her,
I could see her pace of step getting little slower;
As her body was brushed by the gentle breeze,
It blew her sweet fragrance all over my face!

Just one moment, she turned back and smiled;
It was enough to swing my thoughts so wild.
Years passed by, she now will be somewhere
In someone else's arms, may be far or near.

I still keep her close to my heart, near and dear,
And when I see someone who looks like her,
My heart pounds, thoughts can neither bought nor sold,
May be someday I'll see her again – in another world!

Untitled 1...

Muddy shore
cloudy skies
slippery highways
and a wearied mind
that beckons
where is freedom

if one's freedom
let him build
his own prison
what good
is that freedom

free as a bird
if one can
sore in the skies
and build his home
in the clouds

lonely stars
that try to shine
in the evening skies

little boys
flying paper airplanes
that's tossed by the wind
try in vain

old couples
sitting in the park
lost in ages past
life is but a passing dream

slaves to drugs
slaves to passion
beckon
where is freedom

women's voices
lost in cigarette smoke
make
mystic patterns
as a drunken soul

lovers on the beach
lost in fantasy
wait for the day
to exchange their rings

Do You Know…

Do you know, why I am so excited
    To hear your loving voice?
Know why I am so intoxicated
    When your voice brushes my ears?

Though it comes from far away
    Through the air and the phone,
I feel it's here forever to stay,
    With its unique and exhilarating tone!

I feel the gentle caress of your lips,
    Though, in fact it's just the phone!
I could feel, close to me, your presence
    Though you and I are apart and alone.

It brings me wonder at times,
    How all these events came to be;
This meeting of two perfect strangers
    In a small world of you and me!

Though often times quickly it may end,
    Again and again, I long to hear your voice.
Yes, spoken words are hard to find
    To say how much I need you face to face!

Memories...

I had been here,
Yes, I am sure;
I have seen these mountains
And these sparkling fountains;
Yes, I was once lost
In this beauty that will last
Beyond the test of time,
Always keeps the serene rhyme.

Now too I am lost
Not in this beauty at its best;
As I close my eyes
My imaginations reach the skies,
And I am in the threshold
As I try to behold
The vastness of your thoughts
That fills my universe!

Yes, more is the beauty of thee,
More is the tranquility I see;

The beauty of your heart
And the serenity it can depict
Though beyond spoken words
Fulfills my desires and needs.
Yes, I need you now, not in memories,
But for real, fulfilling my desires!

Yesterday Is Gone…

When I showed a few poems I wrote to a friend of mine, she asked me whether I had failure in love. I just smiled! She asked the same question again. I smiled again and said, "Love never fails nor ends; how can I un – love whom I have loved?" And she smiled!!

So many things that I see, whisper your name to me,
So many things that I hear, remind your days with me.
    And yesterday is gone
    Like a snow flake on a leaf,
    What I'm left with for today
    Are the memories of you!

The ripples in the waters and the autumn leaves that scatter,
And the cold wind that blows, bring back your thoughts to me.
    And yesterday is gone
    Like a snowflake on a leaf,
    What I'm left with for today
    Are the memories of you!

Like a lightning in a stormy sky, like a rainbow on a cloudy day,
You left me on our way, and this heart of mine still longs for you.
    And yesterday is gone
    Like a snowflake on a leaf,
    What I'm left with for today
    Are the memories of you!

When the cold storm is over and sweet spring is everywhere,
I wish you come back to me – to make my dreams come true.
    And yesterday is gone
    Like a snowflake on a leaf
    What I'm left with for today
    Are the memories of you!

Waiting for You, My Beloved...

I was watching the moon lit skies
And the golden ripples on the waters;
I was waiting on that sandy shore,
Waiting for you my beloved dear!

On your way my sweet darling,
Who touched your golden ear ring
To make your lovely ear blush,
Is it that cold evening breeze?

Or is it the thought of my lips
Brushing, nibbling gently your ears
That made you close your eyes
In ecstasy surging in your veins!

As the wind brushed your lovely face,
What did it whisper into your ears
To make you blush again all over,
Just like it does when we are together?

My lips are waiting, waiting,
Longing restlessly to meet yours

To taste that sweetest honey;
Yes, I am waiting restlessly!

Is that the moonlight from the sky,
That stopped you briefly on your way?
Was she too jealous of you,
When she saw the beauty in you!

Through those soft clothes of yours,
Did she see the beautiful curves?
I saw you cup your lovely breasts
With your tender fingers!

I am waiting, my beloved daily,
Counting the stars in the galaxy
And to look deep in to your eyes
To hear the stories and the melodies!

Two Worlds Collide...

Turn your face to my side
Let me see it blush!
Let me look into those eyes,
Eyes that I adore so much,
Eyes that look through me
Touching my heart!

Come, come closer to my side,
Let me see you blush!
Let me look into your eyes,
And the stories they tell;
Let me keep on looking
And search deep within!

Come, lay down by my side
Let me feel you blush!
Let me whisper love into your ears;
Two hearts united and broken at times
Trying to bring harmony
When two worlds collide!

Warm Within…

Winter will be dark and cold
    Only for those with no warm memories,
Days will be spring to behold
    For us when we think of those moments;
        The moments we shared our love
        When we gave each other all we have!

It's cold and windy outside,
    But I feel warm with thoughts about you;
Though you are not by my side
    I could feel you, hold you, only you!
        Just as when we shared our love
        And we gave each other all we have!

I wake up in the early morning
    Wanting you to want me the way you do,
I stretch my arm around you bringing
    You closer to my heart, as I always do!
        Just as when we shared our love
        And we gave each other all we have!

Being You...

Thank you for giving you,
Thank you for being you,
You made my life complete
And just with words I can't write
    How much I love you.

As the dawn is to the nights
And as the shore is to the seas,
To you I look forward to
You are my dream come true
    And I love you beyond words

Dancing through my mind,
With fragrance from the autumn wind
Are the sweet moments you gave me
And the memories that came to be
    Part of loving you.

The singing birds tell me you're here,
The rainbow in the sky tells me you're near

And my fleeting mind loves to accept
You are not someone easy to forget
    And my love to you is true.

Sometimes in this beautiful world,
The playground of our loving God
We will find a home of our own
And life's blessings to call our own
    And I hope our prayers be heard.

Waiting to Hear Your Voice…

In vain I did try to reach you
Just to tell you that I miss you;
You weren't there, I was left in despair
This mind of mine needs some repair!

It hasn't been long, but it seems like ages
Since I heard that inspiring voice
That leads me to write my next song
And send it to where it does belong.

It's very late, past fairy's time
I couldn't sleep, losing track of time,
This long wait drives me real crazy
I tell you, loving and waiting aren't too easy.

I search my heart and ask the question
And wait for at least some suggestion;
But then I realize, the answer is your choice
Which I long to hear through your voice!

Failed to Express…

I opened my eyes this morning thinking about you,
    Stretched my arms to hold you close to me;
I realized I was only dreaming about you –
    Thoughts about you kept on surrounding me.

I could still feel the sweet nectar of your lips,
    Your skin's fragrance still intoxicates me, as then,
I could still feel the softness of your lovely breasts,
    I could feel your breath exquisitely mixing with mine!

You were at arm's reach, yet it took so long to find you,
    Felt the magic in your eyes, yet failed to express my desire,
It's like a fairy tale, finally I got to really know you
    And to be blessed with the comfort and warmth so dear!

Everywhere I look, I see your beautiful face,
    Feel your arms comfortably wrapped around my neck.
I long to see that irresistible desire in your eyes
    And to get lost in your love, with no words left to speak!

Missing You…

I realized how much I missed you,
When I heard your voice over the phone.
Am I falling in love with you,
Unable to leave this heart of mine alone?

Am I trying to find someone so dear,
That I have lost to the mercies of fate,
Or is it because you were mine and dear
In another world, in body and spirit?

When you are near, looking into my eyes
A thousand songs are sung within my mind;
Near and dear, yet pulled away by force,
I wish these feelings will have no end.

In a special way you have given some tranquility
For my troubled and worried mind;
Though nothing stays from here to eternity,
I wish you are mine, now that I have found!

In Your Arms…

If you said you love me to please me,
That would be the sweetest lie I ever heard,
But, in my heart I knew you love me,
To me you're the sweetest that ever happened!

Yes, I had to wait, seems like a long time
Until you whispered, "I love you very much!"
I will never be tired of hearing it any time
For each time it's a melody with a new touch.

Oh! How much I wish you are here and near,
So, I could hear your gentle whisper in my ears;
I could see your face blush all over in its splendor,
It seems to me that you have been away for years!

I have lots of sweet memories to cherish,
But my heart desires to make more memories
That will never end—this always is my wish
To be with you, in your arms, in your embrace!

Do You Know…

You know how to speak to my heart,
    Your words can reach my very soul;
How can time and distance keep us apart,
    Now that you have come to fill my all.

Where did you learn the enchanting lyric
    To drive me to the edges of ecstasy?
Where did you learn the rhythm and the music
    That drive me beyond any fantasy?

I close my eyes, I can feel your breath,
    I can feel the pressure of your body!
Again and again, I try to capture this myth
    Only to be lost in the serenity of your beauty!

Words with No Meaning…

Soft as a gentle whisper
Speak softly to me
With words
That make no meaning,
But can create music
Within a drunken heart
That's lost
In the divine beauty
And the desire
In your eyes!

I see the moonlight
Caressing you,
And you move in ecstasy;
Every move reveals
The unblemished shapes
That are meticulously covered!
I see your lips part
Whispering words
That are neither heard
Nor understood.

The shore awaits
For the undying embrace
Of the rolling waters;
The moon woos with the clouds
In unparalleled majesty.
I look at you,
Your eyes penetrate
Through my very soul;
And my spirit merges with yours
With nothing left to lose!

Is It Real or a Dream…

Oh! How much I miss you,
    How much I like to hear your voice.
What is that I find in you,
    That adds such an intoxicating spice?

How long will you keep this silence,
    Not saying the words, I want to hear?
Do you know how often your silence
    Torments me, impossible to bear?

Questions, questions, you may say,
    And I know that you wouldn't answer!
But how can I force and defray
    This search that will go on forever?

I close my eyes, I see the ocean waves
    Ripple, rush and make love to the shores.
The bashful clouds close their eyes
    And try to slip away into the skies.

I see you stepping down from the rainbow
    With arms stretched out towards me.
Distance has no meaning as I see it now,
    You are in my arms, that's enough for me!

A Long Time…

It has been such a long – long awaiting time,
I think you might have forgotten my name!
I remember the pages filled with words of your passion
That reached me like a new dawn across the ocean!

It was a pleasure to see your feelings in the mail,
Among the often unwanted messages in the pile!
It gave me immense pleasure to read them one by one
Over and over again, but now where are they gone?

Have you taken me, forever, out of your mind
Are those memories got lost in the blowing wind?
But I'm still waiting, hoping to hear your voice
And see you coming to me and holding me close!

My Heart Says…

Every now and then, morning and evening time,
    There is only one thought that forever fills me;
Every time do I wake out of a sweet dream,
    There is only one beloved that entwines me!

    My heart says, it must be you,
    Yes, I am sure, it must be you!

When, in the morning, the blue bird sings,
    It echoes only one sweet and adorable voice;
When I see the moon amidst the wandering clouds,
    There is only one lovely face I see that smiles!

    My heart says, it must be you,
    Yes, I am sure, it must be you!

When I am feeling lonely, and think I'm lost,
    There is a beautiful pair of eyes that says it cares;
When I am hurt, and pain penetrates my heart,
    There are two hands that stretch at me to caress!

My heart says, it must be you,
Yes, I am sure, it must be you!

When my heart palpitates with love and affection,
There is a pair of lips that can always quench me;
When I am so much filled with emotion and passion,
There is a darling who can always drive me to ecstasy!

My heart says, it must be you,
Yes, my sweetheart, it must be you!

This Waiting…

Come to me, my moon,
Come to me real soon!
This waiting is hard to endure,
I want to be with you sooner.

Come to me, my song,
Don't tarry so long!
I want to hear you whisper in my ears,
I want to feel your skin against my lips.

Come to me, my symphony,
I'm waiting for that harmony.
If waiting can make one rich and wiser,
How rich and wiser I will be this winter!

It's cold and windy outside,
You make me feel warm inside;
How swiftly the days have gone by,
And this longing is so hard to pass by.

I count the days, count the weeks,
This heart of mine is so restless;
Your love, your words, and your touch
Only have the magic I need so much!

At Arms' Reach...

I called your name this morning
    Hoping that it will reach your ears;
I called your name again this evening
    Hoping, this time it will reach your ears!

But my voice was consumed by the clouds
    That roam with fury in the thundering skies;
May be washed away by the soaring waters
    Of the ocean that separate our shores!

But I do feel in my heart that you heard me;
    I feel that my message has reached your heart,
Since I saw you in my dreams answering me
    The questions I have asked – to the very last!

I know this, it's in my mind very clearly,
    That distance is not as difficult as it seems;
For hearts united as one and beat in harmony,
    One is always at arm's reach, as we close our eyes!

New Meaning...

This new music touches my heart like never before
    Since I found you in my wearied journey,
That took me across the oceans to farther yonder;
    Places I have seen, faces I have forgotten are many.

I never even stopped to think, a moment or two
    That this fairy queen will step into my life,
Touch my heart, feel my spirit, and love me too!
    Yes, life has a new meaning, this is a new life.

Love has to care, love has to wait, and love has to forgive
    As your love has shown me, when I was wrong!
Did I hurt you my sweetheart with words of strife,
    Words that could have ended our beautiful song?

Thank you for being you, thank you for believing;
    When hearts united, they beat in harmony,
Without words, they create music divine,
    Loving is giving, giving is sharing life anew!

Magic of Love...

I love you because I love you,
I need you because I need you;
To be loved by you truly and dearly
Is the best thing that happened to me!

It's so comforting to be with you,
It's so assuring that which you do;
To be lost in your love, to be lost in you
Make my wearied life brand new!

Times are hard, I'm making it through;
Your touch, your kiss, your whisper still do
Have the magic of bringing back to my life
What I have lost in time and strife!

Longing…

I can't get enough of you,
Every moment is something new –
Adds a brand new meaning to love,
Shines a new ray of hope from above!

There is always a need to conquer,
The joy it gives is a sweet surrender,
You may think, I got what I wanted,
But the quest of mine has never ended.

I hear a new melody yet unknown
Every time I hold you as my own,
And every moment we are together,
I wish our belonging lasts forever.

Time and tide never wait for anybody,
As each day slowly or swiftly passes by,
My love to you grows even stronger
Like old wine stored for many a year!

I have willingly let you enter my life,
You have known most of my strife.
I hope you will accept me as I am
And try not to put on me the blame!

Doing without you is the hardest of all,
But thoughts about you fill with a spell,
I close my eyes and feel you by my side,
Longing for the moment to see you beside!

Remember When…

I felt so tired, exhausted and bored,
I felt like I am a hundred – year old,
But thoughts about you made me young
And echoed like a brand new song!

Yes, I need you more and more, and more,
Desire to be with you grows like never before;
Why are you, from me, so far away,
Still how did you enter my life this way?

Do I stir the same feelings you stir in me,
Do you feel the need to be always with me?
Being wanted by you has its own reward,
Makes me think it's the world's best award!

Do you think of the day I first met you,
Do you remember the time I first kissed you?
Do you remember when you said that you love me?
I remember them all, they are so precious to me!

I Need You…

I need you here so much
And I need your tender touch,
I need your loving kiss,
Do you know how much I miss?

I am hurt so much,
There is no way out as such,
In pain does my body drench
Which your embrace only can quench.

Why are you so far away,
Don't you know I have so much to say?
Come to me and comfort me,
Hold me and touch me.

I close my eyes to feel you,
I stretch my hands to reach you,
I open my mouth to feel your lips
And long to be lost in your fragrance.

Be Near to Me…

As the morning sun shines its rays so bright,
    And as a new day dawns out of darkness,
I count the days reassuring our meeting is at sight,
    Another day closer to have you back in my arms!

I watch the clouds pass by in the starlit skies,
    And wonder whether they whisper my message
Into your ears as they make endless patterns;
    Did you watch them too, trying to send your message?

As the cool breeze touches my face and passes by,
    I could feel your fragrance as you softly embrace
Pressing your very nakedness close to my skin, and try
    To let me know the depth of love that none can erase.

A thousand times, my heart echoes the words, 'I miss you,'
    But then it looks for the dawn in the yonder horizon,
Reassuring that by one more day I am closer to you
    To feel you, to kiss you, and to hold you as mine!

Say I Love You…

Hey, it seems like a long time
That I wrote my thoughts in a poem,
Now when I sit and type these words,
I know that I have hidden my feelings!

I want to whisper softly into your ears,
I want to kiss those tempting lips of yours,
I want to quench my thirst by your mouth,
I want you to surround me by your warmth.

All these I want now, though you are far away,
But above all, my dear, I hear you gently, say,
"I love you, and my heart belongs to you!
My love, my true love, how much I miss you!"

Section 2

Dreams

How can we live without dreams? They provide us what we are not able to achieve in reality. Sometimes they can tell what is going to happen. When we accomplish something that we wanted, we say, 'Our dreams come true.' Dreams are synonymous with human life.

Memories and Dreams...

Memories radiate like small fires,
We can sit beside and warm ourselves,
When we're down and cold with despair
And this world seems to disappear.

So are dreams that lead to another world
And thoughts that never surrender to be bound;
These are the greatest gifts to mankind
What else, so fulfilling, can ever be found?

When I'm lost and forlorn, I just close my eyes
And I could feel your warm heaving breasts
Press against my chest, reassuring me,
That you're here and will never leave me!

I could feel your intoxicating fragrance
Surround me, fly me higher to the heavens,
Where the stars dance in the golden skies
To music that cannot be composed of notes!

Reality and Myth

Hand in hand, we sore into the silky clouds,
Smile at the rainbow and kiss the shiny stars.
There is no night or day, dusk or dawn that ends;
Time is eternal, and so are thoughts and dreams.

Breath mixes with breath creating a legacy,
Bodies radiate creating an eternal ecstasy,
And minds are entwined as a divine symphony;
Memories and dreams, Oh! What a perfect harmony!

It's Fairies' Time...

There will be calm after storm
And sunshine after the heavy rain,
Quietness will follow thunder
And rainbows smile from the yonder!

Darkening clouds will vanish from the skies,
Leaving infinite twinkling stars,
Making the land a gleaming beauty
And the landscape will look so pretty!

Quiet and happy are the moments
I spent with you my beloved these days,
Even if they are to end in memories,
I'll cherish – till I die – those memories!

They are the sweetest in my life,
I wish I could be with you all my life
Sharing good times and times of sorrow,
Always waiting for a better tomorrow.

The land sleeps, it's fairies' time,
I'll let you sleep for some more time,
Looking at my lovely sleeping beauty
Lying in solace and comfort beside me!

When sleep takes over me and lie on bed
And I close my eyes, and rest by your side,
I wish I will be dreaming about you
And in the morning, I can share them with you!

Really…

What I really need is to be with you,
What I really feel is to whisper love to you,
What I really wish is to lie down beside you,
What I really hope is that you feel the same way too!

Life is becoming an illusion without you by my side;
Every morning I wake up, longing you next by my side;
With thoughts about you, I begin the toils of the day
And hoping to dream about you till the dawn of the next day!

Why are you so far away, far away from me,
Did you call me last night, I heard you calling me?
I woke up, it was a dream, but dreams came true,
I heard your voice this morning, made me brand new!

Passion surged through, as I got immersed in your voice,
There is nothing in this world, I so much rejoice;
I had to stop, lest emotions go out of control
Which you alone can satisfy and quench all in all!

Dancing Like a Pretty Queen…

I have so many dreams about you,
    Dreams that can never happen in life;
Yes, I have strange dreams about you,
    But sweetheart, without those I have no life!

I dreamed of you dancing like a pretty queen,
    Holding hands, dancing before envious eyes
In a ballet that no one so far has ever seen,
    Yes, you were like a heavenly masterpiece.

When the ballet was over, you were in tears
    You whispered softly, "I love you," in my ears
Tears trickling down your cheeks, wetting your lips;
    I gently kissed you, wiped those tear drops.

I opened my eyes and you were not there,
    With an aching heart I looked around for you,
I could feel your fragrance, hear your whisper
    And I stretched my hands in vain to reach you!

Are They Only Dreams…

Every now and then, when I close my eyes
I hear your voice in my dreams,
And your soft and gentle whispers
Render music and harmony to my ears.
And the stories, your beautiful eyes tell
Create in me an ecstatic spell!

I could feel your fragrance
Penetrate, inspire my senses.
I could see the clouds pass by
Caressing your body.
And the rainbow shining bright
And the birds chirping sweet.

Sound of rain drops falling on the leaves
And the humming rumbling of the bees
Surround my very soul;
All these I could vividly feel!
I stretch my hands to touch
And see if you are at arm's reach.

I could hear your voice
As a distant melody that lingers
Calling my name,
Dreams and thoughts, are they the same?
Am I lost, lost in your thoughts
Or my thoughts transform to dreams?

Maybe I'm a dreamer, that's all I am.
If dreams can bring you home,
Don't wake me;
If I can feel you close to me,
Don't stop me, let me be
For that's the way it came to be!

But then, if that's not your wish,
And if you don't want me to cherish,
But rather let the memories perish
Or from the mind, they slowly diminish,
What is left for me to say
Except that I am left in dismay.

First Distant Sight…

No one ever touched my heart
At the very first distant sight;
That's history when I saw you
And really fell in love with you!
What is the magic in your eyes
Or the enchantment in your voice,
I rather not try to find out,
Exciting as it came about!
Didn't know whether you felt this way,
That's for destiny to convey.
Feelings embedded in the heart
Can reveal, though secretly kept
When you find the one you did seek
No matter how long it may take!

One with Me...

The rays of the morning sun
Shining through the window pane
Woke me up from my dreams;
But dreams come true, it seems

There she was right in front of me,
Pretty, always, only as she can be;
The very nearness of her that early morn
Brought feelings I cannot adjourn.

Her cheek was warm against my lips,
I could breathe the fragrance of her cheeks,
Her body chemistry kept my heart pounding
But then, one has got one's chores pending.

A smile now and then, a sign that I care,
A stop, I'll find time to spare;
Waiting, if waiting makes one wealthy
I won't need any possessions earthly!

Thoughts divine, feelings spiritual
Can be o'er powered by desires physical;
Sweeter than the nectar of rose distilled,
They fill you, to be fulfilled!

She was close – too close to fill my heart
And nothing I could think can take her apart;
I still feel the softness of her breast
This feeling, I can never ever put to rest.

I wish I could hold on to the warmth,
Bury my face, and take a deep breath,
Rest my ear closely on her tender chest
And hear every sound of her heart beat.

Thinking of her gives me utmost joy,
I wish my thoughts could fly high
And reach her in physical forms,
Embrace her, hold her in my arms!

And she be one, one with me,
Cling on to me, be one, one with me!
And she be one, one with me,
Cling on to me, be one, one with me!

End My Dreams...

Sometimes when I am lost in my dreams,
    Lost in my thoughts searching for the unknown,
When Heaven closes on me its golden doors
    And I am wandering, lost and forlorn
Not knowing whether to ask for forgiveness
    Or to surrender, and toss all I have away,
I believe, this is the way, and not to lose the bliss
    That by destiny, brought to me, along the way.

I do not want to stop and question
    And search to find, it's right or wrong,
She has filled my thoughts and imagination
    And without her, I'll be an unwritten song;
Time alone will tell how strong is this bond,
    A day may come when she will end my dreams;
I won't complain if that be near at hand
    I'll blame it on destiny that brought her in the first place!

These Are My Dreams...

Thou art not mine,
I am not thine
Yes, I know that,
But, why is it then
My heart beats fast
When I see thy sweet face?

Sweet are the moments
I sat by your side talking to you;
Like the nectar of rose distilled
Time passes with bliss when I'm with you!
The warmth I feel on my heart
Looking at your beauty
And your angelic face is serene!
You are different, such a loving person,
I know that!

Days follow nights and seasons change,
The tides keep on merging with sands
In their endless search for harmony,
Leaves fall, only to bloom in splendor,
The wheels of tome never stop to roll!

But, within the time we have in hand,
I wish if only you are mine.
I know I have miles and miles to go
Before I sleep, a long task to do
Before my journey is done, but I'm sure
The warmth and affection you can give
Can keep me going
With spirit rejuvenated
And ambitions cherished!

You will adorn the garden of my heart
With a rose that is the most pleasant
In its fragrance,
With a lily that's the purest of all
And a daisy
With its petals, the loftiest I have seen!

But, these are my dreams,
I wish, if only you could read
My mind and its thoughts
And its emotions and feelings
When it thinks about you.
You too will, then feel,
That you belong to me.
And I'll be the happiest in mind and soul!

Do You Know My Dreams...

I stretch my hands to reach the stars
    Like a child trying to catch the rainbow,
I stretch my thoughts, but where are the words?
    Where they hide from my sight, I do not know!

You wished that my dreams would come true;
    Do you know my dreams, knowing will you wish the same?
For in my dreams, I have said, "I love you!"
    A thousand times and called out your name.

I have a million stories to tell you
    If only you are at my arms reach,
Spoken words cannot express how much I adore you,
    The right words are beyond my fancy's reach!

Let me stop here and wait for another time,
    The time it takes to know your thoughts
Till I can find the right words that rhyme
    And words that can express harmony of hearts!

The Music and Your Fragrance…

The music was playing – in the beach – soft and low,
    Sometimes the voices were loud, but there was harmony,
You were beside me, I could see your eyes glow,
    The music of your smile seemed like a perfect symphony!

Your eyes penetrated through the periphery of my heart,
    Your own fragrance reached the depths of my senses!
Have I known you – really known you in the past
    Maybe in another world, another life, close in presence!

Did you see me the way I saw you, did you feel the same?
    Every moment was precious, one step in the long search –
To be loved, to be touched, to be admired – does this sound sane?
    There was this feeling, this desire, which in vain I tried to reach.

Your every movement, your every word reminded me
    Of someone I was looking for in a long long time;
Maybe destiny brought you to me, I have yet to see,
    But I know, for my poetry you are the words and rhyme!

We met only to part, but we met to love and to be loved,
    Love never dies, in some way it lives in our minds!
The night we spent away from the crowd under the cloud
    Was bound to happen for we were united by destiny's hands!

It is dreamer's time, dark outside, I close my eyes to sleep,
    But you are there vivid and clear, just like the other night!
If it is a dream don't wake me up, let me dream and sleep,
    If it is a thought, I'll think about you for the rest of the night!

Dreams...

Somewhere in a tiny island
Where the palm leaves sway
In harmony with the blowing wind –
Wish you were there with me my love.
Could I then hide my feelings,
If that be our wish?
I can refrain from those songs,
But how can I stop my dreams?
If dreams are only to be dreamt,
How good are they?
Like a flower that lost its nectar,
Withered and dry, they fade away;
And so would those dreams,
Lo, I couldn't let it happen.
Those dreams should be realities
Of love shared between us!

Words Made No Meaning...

Thank you for being there when I needed you the most,
Thank you for holding me when I felt I was lost
And providing me the assuring comfort against your breast,
Making me feel like a lost bird that finally found its nest!

Yes, my love, I like to share the little things with you,
The little things that made this life of mine a question without clue,
But the story is long, too long to put them in words here,
I wish you are here that I could whisper gently in your ears!

My journey has been a struggle, but often blessed with rainbows
That brightened my life, but seldom were a permanent bliss;
Though I was surrounded with laughter around, I felt lonely,
Trapped in events that I neither liked nor understood really!

Words made no meaning when I wanted them to be heard,
My aching heart often said I should listen to my head,
But here I am, as I was, as I ever would be – a dreamer
Dreaming of flying in the skies with you as my follower!

Hey, What Are You Thinking…

You constantly fill my thoughts,
    Nothing else registers in my memory;
I see you in the starlit nights,
    As the moon that brings harmony!

I wonder what you're thinking now,
    Hey, my distant moon who came to me;
Willing, hesitant, yet with a distinct glow,
    I need you by my side, touching me!

My fingers long to caress your soft skin,
    My lips wait to taste your lip's nectar,
I like to see your face closer lifting your chin
    And to you, and you alone I wish to surrender
        — if only in my dreams!

Section 3

Friends

During my younger days and in adult life, I have met a lot of people-some became friends, some stayed as acquaintances and some, I never met them at all afterwards. I had moments to share their joy, fun, pain, their problems and frustrations. Sometimes I wonder what's going through in their hearts.

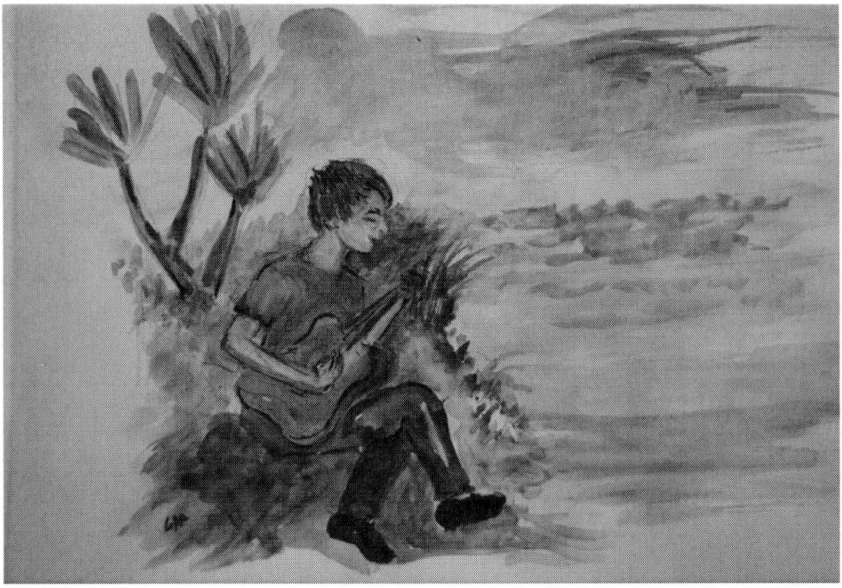

If I Could Share His Song…

I was walking along the Galveston Beach in Texas. I saw a young man sitting by the shore and playing a sad tune with his guitar. I wished I could share his sorrows and I wrote this.

I saw him sitting by the Galveston shore
Lost deep in the melody of his guitar;
A sad song came from him as a mourning wind
As the foaming waters made endless patterns around.

I saw him looking at the crawling foam
As if there is no place for them to call home;
I could see deep contempt in his eyes
As he stared farther and yonder at the seas.

Maybe here at the very golden shores
He had spent many blissful evenings
Watching the divine beauty of the setting sun
And felt the warmth of his beloved one.

Maybe here at the very golden shores,
He gently whispered words of love in her ears;

For the first time, he gently kissed her lips
And felt the happiness that true love brings.

Maybe in the course of time, I do not know
He lost her to someone else he never knew,
And found her in his arms at this very shore;
Felt the pain in his heart grow more and more.

Maybe here at the very sandy shores,
He played with his friend from his class
And found what true friendship can bring,
Sharing stories and jokes and a song

And maybe these cruel tides, rising high with foam
Took his friend away from him as they swam,
Fancy free just enjoying the cool blue water,
Only to come back alone to the empty shore.

I know not what made him sing such a sad song,
But I know something has gone so wrong;
There is agony in his heart, and the shore and the seas
Seem like everlasting silent witnesses to his woes.

It is not my intent to know his story
Nor to stop him playing that sad melody,
But I wish, somehow, I could ease his pain
And if I could, make him happy again.

Precious Moments…

Part of a closing speech at an international conference

There is music and laughter in the air,
The tinkling of wine glasses makes a melody;
Science is forgotten for a moment,
Oh! How enlightening is this to the soul!

The equations we solved, the computations we made
And the measurements, all will fade away one day;
The day we retire from this pursuit of science.
Yet there is more to life than science can offer!

When the journals and the papers we wrote
Are forgotten as long-lost dreams.,
These precious moments we spend together
Will linger on in our hearts forever.

But my mind is not here, it's on time machine
Traveling along the roads I have been,
Seeing the faces and places I have forgotten
But reminding the impact they made in my life!

My First Friend…

I was only four years old and she too was four;
She was my very first friend, I had none before.
We were together in that old nursery school
And we used to sit together on the parapet wall.

One day she wetted her underwear and the floor,
The teacher was furious, made her clean the floor
And sent her out through the class room door;
I haven't seen her cry like that ever before.

I took her hand and led her towards the garden,
Touched her face, wiped her tears – memories are golden!
We sat there together a long time, talked and talked,
But I don't remember a single word that we muttered.

The wheels of time rolled on, and we met once again
She was beautiful, she was married to a friend of mine;
I thought about the days we played together in the garden,
Those hugs of innocence and moments of admiration.

I close my eyes now, and saddle on my time machine,
I could see all my old friends pass by smiling;
One by one the pages of my book – my life – unfold,
I see her face, and those sweet memories never become old!

Since I Said Good Bye…

Thoughts about you filled my mind
As the airplane sheared through the wind.
Gentle on my mind were also the thoughts
About the laughter and the music in the nights.

I am back to my home, where I belong;
It seems that it has been so long,
Since I said, "good bye" to you.
Needless to say that I love to hear from you.

This is my wish on your anniversary
That health and happiness prevail every day.
My special love to your daughter and son
And a special wish for us to meet again.

How Can I Forget...

We were driving from Kanpur to Varanasi, India (1969). I met this man on the way, who touched my heart like no one before!

Once in your lifetime, you come across that someone
Who could, like no one else, make a lasting impression!
It was a sunny late morning, we were on our way
From Kanpur to Varanasi on that pot-holed dusty highway;
Six of us, Bill and Helen Riley from Iowa State University,
Me, the driver, and Juneja and Gopal from the vicinity –
All set to see the holy place, have a dip at Triveni Sangam
The taxi bumped up and down amid the sun's scorching beam!

Our mouths dried, longed for a place where we can find
Some fruits or a glass of water, and lo it seemed like God-send,
There was this lean man in ragged clothes with a table beside
And freshly picked fruits from the tree that was by the roadside;
"Can we buy some fruits from you?" I asked him in a gentle voice,
"No sir," came his reply, as he stared, from head to toe, at
    my friends.
In shock as I looked at him, with a smile he started to say,
"These fruits are free for travelers like you who come
    from far away!"

As we tasted those delicious fruits, there came a boy running to us,
And I stretched my hand to give him a fruit, which he did refuse!
"No sir," the father said, "This tree was planted by my grandfather
Only to bear fruits that satisfy the need of a stranger or traveler;
God has provided me a small piece of land behind my hut, wisdom
    to know,
Hands to sow, rain for the crop to grow, and a son to take over
    when I go."
So that was his mission, I felt so humble before this man, realized
    how low
Am I before his heart so big and so humane, as I watched his
    eye's glow.

Ram (that's his name) led us to his small hut, introduced his wife to us
Who seemed to bring another baby to this world in couple of months!
As Dr. Riley offered him some money to take care of his family,
He flatly refused, for he won't see again the man from a foreign
    country
And for sure, before his journey ends, to pay back him the money!
I placed some money on his hand, reassured, "I'm not far from
    you, you see
At another time I can get back the money, so you won't have any more
    debts!"
And as I hugged him to say good bye, I could see tear drops in his eyes.

I could never forget Ram for a long time, he was right in front of me
That lean, short man in torn clothes, and the words he spoke to me;
But it's his kindness and his care for others that touched my heart!
I spoke of him in several meetings as the most important person
    I ever met

In my life – which I said with pride and truthfulness from within.
It has been more than forty years since I met him on that unforgettable morn,
I could not see him again as I told him then, not sure if he is in this world,
But as I type this, tears from my eyes prevent me from seeing the keyboard.

Recently, I happened to drive on the same road again and looked for the place where I met Ram. Everything has changed completely. There are new coffee shops along the way and Ram's cottage is gone. I wonder what happened to Ram and his family. I wasn't even sure whether Ram is still in this world. I felt a deep agony in my mind.

My Love It's You….

That was our first Christmas party in my graduate school years. I wrote this on the nice large napkin on the table. My classmate Dr. Marianne Scott gave a copy to me years later during a conference!

Everything looks tranquil and serene
And the soft lights and the warmth of music
Bring to my mind and body a feeling supreme,
I look at thee while my fingers caress
The divine softness that holds the nectar,
Oh! my love thou art a masterpiece of art!

Is it jaaz or the beat of the drum
That gives a rhythm in my heart,
Or is it the sweet laughter
That comes from the lips of the girls around,
I wonder what it could be – it's you my love
Gleaming between those shining crystals!

Smiling at me, giving me pleasure un bound
And tinkling to lead me to ecstasy,
When I feel alone – though I am not alone

And forlorn; it's you my beloved,
My love and my friend – it is you
Scotch on the rocks!

– written when sober!

Friendship…

Four days ago, we did not know each other,
Science brought us together,
But music, songs, and poetry made us friends
And with each other, we set the world's problems apart.
As music filled the air
Friendship and love filled our hearts.
Every meeting has a time to end!
So, friends,
As we say good-bye, we say so
Not as scientists, but as friends.
We shared a laughter or two
And at times we cried!
But as we go back to our homes
We will remember, from Russia with love.
As good wine, our friendship will grow with time!
Until we meet again we cherish these moments.
When we meet, we'll share our laughter one more time!

Is It Real…

Sometimes you meet someone in unexpected place, whose memory doesn't fade away. She is one such person – not easy to forget.

Though surrounded, I was feeling lonesome,
Pain that I cannot explain took control of me,
Didn't know where and when I can find the shore
From the troubled waters that rise high all over.

There was music, wine and sparkling lights,
Cigarette smoke made endless mystic patterns,
Folk's laughter, hugs and whispers, and the rest,
None could take away the pain that filled my heart.

She took me by her hands, led me to the dancing floor
The love song that was played was pleasing to the ear,
Gently she pressed her silky cheek against mine
As we danced to the music, that sounded divine!

"You look sad", said she, slowly kissing my cheek,
I looked at her though the ambience was rather dark;
She was really so beautiful, and it felt so soft
As she pressed her lovely breast against my chest!

Reality and Myth

I wished that the dance would last forever,
The music stopped, followed one by a rocker.
As we sat back, she put her arms around me,
Slowly I felt that the pain was leaving me.

We spoke a lot, hugged a lot, and kissed a lot,
She said she was happy that we could meet;
I told her she was very nice and beautiful,
She said I'm handsome and also very special!

Added she, my name was beautiful, she won't forget
And will remember me every single moment.
I kissed her good bye with a heartfelt, 'thank you
For easing my pain and make me feel brand new'!

I was sitting in the airplane bound for home;
As time passed by, I started to feel lonesome,
My thoughts drifted; as I closed my eyes
I could still feel her body against mine and her kiss.

I opened my eyes and thought about the reality
Of life, love, meeting and parting all in entirety;
Maybe now, she will be dancing with someone else
And say the same words she uttered to bring me solace.

Maybe she is kissing him, telling him he is handsome
And ask him to remember her when he gets home
For she is a dancer, paid to dance with her clients
Who visit the bar, spend some time paying the price!

A deep sigh came from within, I could not stop
Thinking about her, the wet feeling of her lip,
The softness of her breasts, her gentle caress,
And her words, but above all the look in her eyes!

As You Travel…

Just a brief note to let you know,
That when to another country you go,
These are my sincere wishes for you
To grant the best in what you do!

You will be in my thoughts dear
And you too will feel that I am near,
And as the new task ahead, you endure,
There will be time later for you to share.

So, have a nice, joyful and safe trip,
Take care, and have a good night's sleep;
And as the harvest of your work you reap
I like to share your success, for me to keep!

Friends...

I wrote this during a dinner party (August 12, 2000) on a paper napkin that was on the table. Paul took that paper and later sent it back to me with the following note:

Gabriel,

I very much enjoyed hosting the meeting, and spending time with one another. In many ways we are coming together as a family. It was nice for Jill to finally meet you, having heard so much about you these last few years. Your napkin note was remarkable, and I have copied it below. You had Jill in tears as she reread it on the way home... very dear. Thank you for everything. You have been kind in so many ways.

My best
Paul

Sorry, I broke our usual tradition,
    No joke, no poetry, not rightfully done;
But here we are, it's sort of compensation,
    Here we are, sharing these moments of relaxation.

This is the most diversified group I can find!
    There is Jill, the sweet lady, who brightens this table
With a smile and laughter beautifully blended
    And here is Sergey, the master of jokes – enjoyable.

Ahmed is here, lost his camel, but not his jokes,
    Makes this place lively, for a male audience
And Nickolay, the master of ceremonies, a vodka he needs,
    I am caught in between, master of none, but jack of all trades!

Yulu in front, a go getter, often with words forbidden,
    Ken, a wolf in sheep's clothing, enjoys these jokes;
Oh! There is Victor, the new Russian, with dollars his pocket is laden,
    But most of all, there is Paul, my friend from Mars!

    I think I have it all!!

How Can I Forget – The Tsunami…

Ram was the most unforgettable person in my life,
But then came Ayyappan, the taxi driver;
I met Ram in North India with my two American friends;
I didn't think at that time that I will one day settle
    back in the U.S.
As I sit here and started to write about Ram the farmer,
I cannot stop thinking and write about Ayyappan the driver.

Visiting India and see our family members and friends
Gave me and my wife a joy that cannot be expressed by words,
Though the roads were winding and dusty with potholes,
We found Ayyappan manage to drive with such a skill!
The more times we have been driving on his old taxi cab,
The idea of hiring a newer taxi never occurred to us.

The last time we drove in his taxi, a coconut fell on the hood
As a climber dropped the coconuts without any notice
From the tree that was hovering over the middle of the road.

Ayyappan thanked God for no one was hurt nor nothing bad
   happened;
With the already worn out car further damaged, he assured,
"Next time, you come sir, I will have a new car for you indeed!"

Another year passed by, this time I went alone to India – to the south,
It was only a few days after the Tsunami, which hit the south;
I called Ayyappan, no one answered his cell phone,
I thought he must be busy, on his trip to some place with clients;
I called Ayyappan the next couple of days also – with no response.
That evening I saw a newspaper used to wrap something I bought.

As I flipped the pages, I found Ayyappan's picture and a news clip.
In the new car he promised me he was going to buy before our
   next trip
Ayyappan took a family from North India to Kanyakumari,
The father went to the sea shore and onto the waters with his son,
Leaving his pregnant wife with Ayyappan for her to do shopping;
Destiny had it a different way, Tsunami hit the shores of Kanyakumari.

The giant waves came hovering like a monster in fury
In a wink of an eye reaching the shopping area, where they stood,
The waves have already devoured the father and son to their grave.
Those around shouted at Ayyappan to run back for safety.
At that moment his conscience would not allow him to leave
The poor lady carrying a child in her womb to the marching waves.

Ayyappan ran to her, pulled her hands dragging her to safety,
But lo, it was too late, the killer waves consumed him and the lady
And swallowed them down to the deep waters far away.

Yes, he lost his life in trying to save another life, the life of a
> helpless lady,
The new car – his dream was also swallowed with him;
When I think of him, I cannot cry, my tears have dried within.

I just close my eyes and think of those like Ram and Ayyappan
And thousands like him who have loving hearts like theirs,
Caring to the extent of giving their own lives, expecting nothing in
> return,
But their lives are soon forgotten, most of them not even remembered
While those who sell their beauty for fame, wealth for recognition,
Power for glory, corruption for comfort become heroes and heroines!

I think of the vanity of human wishes and the paths to achieve those,
I think of the hatred and jealousy that have taken over mankind;
The unwanted wars and killings, that make no sense, make me shiver.
I wish and pray that a day may come that everyone realizes
That we are all part of a large family, rich and poor, black and white,
But all tied with a supreme bond – the bond of being a human.

Going Away...

Written while in Kanagawa, Japan

With every minute passing, I'm going miles away from you,
    But the precious moments linger near, always quiet and clear
I wish I could hold you close to me, and say the words to you,
    You are a symphony, the words, the rhyme and the melody, dear!

It was such a short time, I feel I have known you for ages
    As if we have met in another world in another life time,
Strange it may seem, yet so familiar is your beautiful face
    As if I have touched and caressed it till the end of time.

Some are bound to meet, a few are bound to stay close,
    It's a mystery no one knows or understands!
I have been a dreamer, dreaming to find true solace,
    You came along, made my days brighter beyond spoken words!

Days In Nagoya...

Written at the closing ceremony of a meeting in Nagoya (December 17, 2001)

As scientists we met, discover our venture,
Share our dreams, share our adventure;
But friends, the papers and articles we write,
The text books and the patents to our credit
Are only vanishing dreams, lost in time;
And when we retire, try to find some rhythm
And explore meaning to our very existence,
These moments we share never lose essence!

In the music that fills the air and the ambience,
There is a friendship that found new existence
And as the liquor fills our nerves and thoughts,
Only one thing remains, it's friendship my friends!
Friendship that passes beyond any barrier
Of color, race, language or any human endeavor,
But one that fills our minds and dearly stored
To remember the days in Nagoya that we shared!

Dear Beverly...

My wife's friend Beverly's mother passed away. I wrote this as message from my wife to Beverly.

Sometimes, in life, God takes away
The greatest gift He has given us;
Sometimes we are left in dismay
And feel that darkness surrounding us.

We feel this emptiness all around,
Speak aloud, but our voice is seldom heard,
Hurt and sorrow all come abound
With no response to that often-spoken word.

Yes, it truly hurts within the most
When you lose your best, your mother;
Yes, I had been through it
Time doesn't heal, the scars don't soften.

But there is one hope that helps us carry on
Our Father, He never fails in His words;
There is His promise that the soul lives on
And one day, together we all will find peace.

I know the pain you are going through'
I couldn't say it in words how I feel;
So I want to let you know this way
That your thoughts, daily my prayers will fill.

May He bestow you with His peace
That you may carry on with your future ahead;
And her spirit be your divine solace
To give you strength, and bring back joy abound.

With prayers
Vimala

When I Was Young…

In July 2000, I participated as the sponsor of an International Symposium. My colleagues know that I write poetry. So they asked me to start my opening lecture with a poem. And I wrote this.

When I was young, I loved to paint,
I used to think, I was born to paint;
Then I thought I was born to be a poet,
I found joy in putting words, the rhyme they create,
It was a great feeling to see young girls cry
When I read those lines, which I called poetry!

My restless mind was still searching for an answer,
I was wondering whether it's crave for literature
Or to leave a permanent shape to my imagination
And my emotions – sculpture was an answer to my passion!

But lo, life doesn't take the course you love to choose
The least I dreamed of or wanted was science!
But that seemed to be my destiny, as it came to be
But I cannot complain, science has been good to me.

I was nothing on my own, but surrounded by friends
With bright intellectual minds dedicated to science,
Only, I had to bring them together and create a bond
Like the fiber that ties beautiful flowers into a garland.

Scientific miracles happen when such minds work together,
Science is a tool to serve humanity, make this world better
Where nationality, color, race or religion is no barrier;
We meet, discuss, argue and plan means for all to prosper.

As I take these long flights back towards my sweet home
I still think and wonder, just as I used to do all the time,
How nice it would be to throw a pebble in a still pond
And watch the ripples grow reach the shore far beyond!

I wonder how nice it would be, just to watch the stars
Twinkling endlessly, and the moon dancing among the clouds,
Soaking my feet in the foaming water, brushed by the sand,
Hear the bird's melody without any written lyrics till my end.

If only I can do all these with you all!

To Rosy…

The Jacobs moved next door as our neighbors when we built our first house.
We became close friends and had a wonderful life.

It was a bright and sunny evening in Thiruvananthapuram,*
I was inspecting the site for construction of our new home;
I heard a car stop nearby, and a very beautiful lady
Fashionably dressed, tiptoed down the unpaved alley.

I greeted the man who drove the car, and said hello,
He waived his hands, and as the lady turned to go
To the next lot, I noticed how amazing she was to look at
With the saree tucked so low exposing her lovely waist.

I guessed they will be our neighbors when we move in,
And so it happened, they moved in with their children;
Our children became friends of theirs as if they knew long before
And brought in news about the uncle and aunt next door.

As months passed by, our acquaintance changed to friendship
Then to a true lasting friendship – as a treasure to keep.

---

*   A City in India, Capital of the State of Kerala

Our families shared together many precious moments
And time has no power to erase those wonderful events.

I used to call her Rosy, and I was the only one to call her
By that name, which she said it was so sweet to hear.
A caring person such as her, in my life I never have met,
Her friendship and love were sincere, pure and from the heart.

I remember the days when she showed her wish so sincere
That I should go abroad to study, come back as a great engineer
And came forward to provide the funds needed to apply
From the money she saved from her expenses day after day!

Her another wish, I could not fulfil, her wish that I will be on my way,
Come back home to lead our lives again, seeing each other every day;
Yes, we had occasions to meet, times to speak, moments to share,
Yet, only in thoughts we could be together, meetings became rare.

Decades passed by, our hairs became gray, years became dearer,
She said, "Now it's time to come back, don't wait too long let's be
 together,
When all of us can have our old life sharing our joy and happiness;"
Maybe it is too late, maybe it is too long, so quickly time passes!

Destiny has its own way, neither be stopped nor questioned,
She lost her husband – just as a bright candle is put off by the wind,
He breathed his last while playing cards, the game he loved,
As he often said, "I wish to die while I stretch my hand to lay
 my card!"

Yes, his life was over the way he wished, but what about her life?
I saw the sorrow hidden in her heart, the desperation of a lonely life
And the anguish hard to quench, left alone in this world to face,
Knowing not what to do and how, live only by His amazing grace.

Yes, it is time that we have to make her happy, be with her more,
Try our best to relieve her mind that is, with all the worries, so sore,
Talk to her in length, and assure her that we are here to give her
    comfort;
With this in mind, I sat down to call her hoping soon we could meet.

No one knows when tragedy strikes, we are fragile as a castle
    made of sand,
The news from the other side of the world over the phone stilled
    my mind;
Rosy is gone, gone forever from this world, gone to her Master's haven,
Just the previous day – alone she came, and alone she was bound to
    Heaven.

I broke this sad news to my wife, she sat still with tears trickling down,
She lost her best friend, a friend with whom she could share
    her pain;
On occasions, together they used to tease me and enjoy my awkward
    smile,
Solemn mood took over her for several days, I knew how she did feel.

I could not cry, my sorrow was beyond tear drops, it choked me
    somewhere,
I was lost in thoughts about Rosy, and all those I wanted for so long to
    tell her

In just a few days when I planned to meet her, be with her and
　　comfort her;
Though too late, still be able to offer support and lasting consolation
　　to her.

At each touch of my fingers on the key board, my mind is flying back
To those days of our lives with Rosy, the days when I was sick,
How she took care of me, the tender and loving care she did bestow
And how the life of this beautiful person has gone like a rainbow.

Rosy, your beautiful face is in front of me vivid and clear to my eyes,
Though the tear drops prevent my vision, I could see those smiles
And the words you spoke so clearly as whispers in my ears;
Will I be worthy enough to see you again, in Heaven, face to face?

To You Kazimierz…

It's a chill breezy night in Krakow,
But my friends around me gave me warmth!
After couple of failed attempts,
This is my first trip to Krakow –
At the hotel, I was pleased by a handshake with warmth,
"Welcome friend," said Kazimierz,
Looked as if he has known me for years!
Just one look, that's all it takes even for friendship.
Thank you, Kazimierz, you made me feel at home,
Often science trails behind human relationship!
Yes, science was spoken these days, thoughts shared,
But a time will come then we all will be tired of science!
But certain things will stand the test of time
Like the times we shared now, the laughter,
The good food and conversations,
Above all our mutual care!

Attending meetings was part of my life for two decades,
Some I remember, some are long forgotten!
But moments I shared, like this,
Such friendly conversation with you

Or the walk in the bone-chilling cold night with my hand
Sharing the warmth of friend's affectionate hands,
The moments we got to share our personal life –
These are treasures, one will always cherish!

As I Recall…

Writing poems in scientific meetings has become a norm in my professional life. My colleagues wanted to hear more from me. This one is from Sochi.

It has been a rather quiet and calm night,
The lingering landscape seemed far from sight;
Yet the soothing rumbling of the Black Sea water
Added an upbeat, harmonious melody to the air.

I was surrounded by friends from far and near
I met during the pursuit of science year after year,
There were new smiling faces and wild laughter
And the world's problems did not seem to matter!

We shared our dreams, laughed at our old and new jokes,
So quickly faded away are the past short four years
When we sat at this very shore, may be with few others;
I could still remember those evenings and the ambience!

It has been fifteen years, the first time I set my foot in this country,
Never even imagined, that for me, there will be another journey
In this direction, not to mention this rubble-filled sea shore,
But each trip brings a new meaning that wasn't there before!

The old melodies from the saxophone took me back fifteen years
And relive in length and breadth those beautiful moments
That added a new source of inspiration to my imagination,
It's true, good memories can erase the pain of frustration!

As I have said before, it's science that brought us together,
But it's the friendship we shared that brought us closer;
Yes, a time will come when the papers we write will not matter,
But the good times we shared, and the memories will not shatter!

To a Good Friend...

I met Mrs. Pat Rhudy when I was a student in graduate school. We talked about poetry, and I wrote this for her.

I love those who love poetry
And when I sit by your side
And lost in the thoughts of those masters
Who have brought life eternal to simple words,
I wish someday, I'll write my best
Which will make you cry
And those tear drops of yours are my gifts to you
For the inspiration you have kindled in my mind!

When I am lost in my thoughts,
I feel there is a doorstep that leads to my home
And this home of yours, is my home
Away from home!
And I wonder when the day comes
When I leave this home towards mine,
The same tear drops will make me blind
As in the day, I left my home!

I know meetings are to end in parting;
Thunder follows lightning,
The thunder is strong,
But I feel weak when I leave friends!
I feel empty
When I leave whom I love,
If emptiness can bring happiness
Then, I will be the happiest!

A strange picture comes to mind. I see you surrounded by your grandchildren. And you read this to them. And talk to them about a friend who was there long time ago! I wonder how you would feel.

Dear Ms. Kathy Tyson...

Written what my wife wanted to convey to her boss as she left.

It was not too long ago it seems that you interviewed me,
I still remember your smile, when you let me in to the room.
Well, months and years have passed by so quickly,
And I recall with joy the happy moments I had with you.
You have taught me, guided me, advised me, but above all
You helped me create the confidence in me and what I did.
I want to say, "Thank you," from the bottom of my heart
With mixed feelings of joy and sorrow, I should say –
Joy that you found a way that will make you build a better career
Sorrow that I will be missing you in the days and months ahead
I wish you God's guidance in whatever you do in your new place
And health, happiness in measures spoken words cannot say!

Best wishes and warm regards,
Vimala

Gone to the Yonder…

During my pursuit of science, I met Boris a truly accomplished engineer. He is gone now.

He was a great friend
    And it makes me wonder
When I say 'was' a great friend –
    He has gone to the yonder
To be one with the One
    Who holds the world in His hands.

Ever since he has been gone,
    He has left this emptiness behind
Which can ever be filled by none
    For he was unique, so hard to find;
Thoughts about him fill my heart,
    Oh! How I wish he is still here.

    We miss you Boris.

Few Words of Farewell...

I found this note written on the paper napkin on the dining table during the farewell ceremony of my Associate Director on his retirement (March 01, 1994), and read it before the audience. Now I am retyping it after a long time.

It appears, it was long time ago,
Yet not too far away,
I walked by 800 North Quincy Street.
I saw a man wearing spectacles,
And in shorts and stockings up to his knees,
With a pipe neatly tucked in his stocking,
Kneeling down on the side walk.
I wondered, 'what's this place I am coming to?'
As I looked down, I was stuck with wonder
At the meticulous care this person showed
To the tulips, plucking the weed away.
I said to myself – he is a hell of a gardener!

Days passed by, nay months, it's government;
I was hired by ONR, and I was back.
Here was the same man to greet me again!

"Welcome," he said with an unforgettable smile,
"I have a piece of advice for you,
So far you have been writing top quality science,
Otherwise you wouldn't be here;
Now you have to write a lot of b…s…,
But make sure, they are top quality!"
Gordon, You are an unforgettable friend in my life;
Now as you set sail for new waters,
Carefree, with more time to spend with nature,
I wish you all the best, God's Blessings,
And life, the way you love it to be!

Out of Control…

Written at the opening ceremony of a conference in Moscow, July 2, 2002.

Detonations are unpredictable
And very often out of control –
Very hard to initiate and sustain;
This effort that seemed so insane
Has changed, now I see rays of hope,
Seeds sown carefully begin to reap –
The fruits of research are sweet
And strengthen as we so often meet!

Do we want the pursuit to compete?
Or with one accord try to collaborate
To reach our goal and destination,
I mean engines flying by detonation
As all our intellects are put in unison
And knowledge shared in discussion
The final yield is the right methodology
To utilize science into technology!

Oh! Flint How Much You Suffer…

It touches my heart and make me cry when I hear about the tragedy going on in Flint. It is a pity that not much is being done when so many other less humane events get so much attention. I wonder how this could be allowed to happen in the first place. (February 2016)

Oh! Flint, the city blessed by God a century ago,
    With bustling factories, schools and churches,
Where folks were busy as the days and nights glow;
    As the raw metals were transformed into engines,
Fitted into attractive automobiles coming out in a row,
    People clapped their hands with joy and laughter
Enjoyed the evenings, danced to the songs so mellow
    And had good night's sleep after a thankful prayer.

Corporations had conscience in those years,
    Those who administer cared about those who toil for bread!
The city was booming, and all lived in heavenly peace
    And Flint was truly blessed as the city to live indeed.
Sometimes man's greed is so hard to understand

And his care for fellow man gets so tarnished,
As years passed by, those in power completely changed
   Although Flint's working people remained unchanged.

Corporations lost their conscience, focused only on wealth,
   Jobs got shifted to nearby countries for a cheaper price;
The city lost its charm and gradually its own worth,
   Poverty, scarcity of jobs and depression took their place;
Those in power forgotten their solemn duty bestowed,
   Ego and selfishness took over their rotten conscience,
Racism and supremacy self-proclaimed dominated;
   Alas, the city was abandoned, as if no one knew its presence.

When money mattered over peoples' very existence,
   A few elected and appointed officials became just like animals
With no compassion on the others as their hunger they ease;
   Yes, Flint became a ground for the powerful to eat the helpless!
In a country that boasts of its wealth, prosperity and power,
   Flint became part of a third world country or even less;
Where in the world can you find a city with poisoned water
   Or the cries and the plea of the people reaches only
     deaf ears?

Poisoned water fed in pipes to save money for the city or to the rich,
   Officials who bring out the truth are condemned as lunatics
And doctors who strive to save children are ignored of their speech,
   Can we allow children left to die due to rotten acts
     of politics?

It's not a disease that can be cured by a bottle of capsules
    Or a course of injections that can cure the damage done
        to our kids!
Are we ignoring another Hiroshima with children born with diseases,
    That can neither be cured nor controlled affecting coming
        generations?

It seems some portion of our society has lost its sanity,
    A crying child's voice (out of pain) is seldom respected or
        heard;
Those in power want more power and seek after vanity,
    And the mother's plea for a dying child is often ignored.
Do these hypocrites think that their blood is thicker than the rest,
    That the poor can be easily bought and sold – it's just insanity,
They will have to answer to the one above us one day at last,
    But, we have to act as human beings and are here to save
        humanity.

Born to Paint...

Written during a dinner in a conference amidst several toasts, St. Petersburg, July 10, 2003.

When I was young, I loved to paint,
I used to think, I was born to paint;
In those years, paints were hard to find,
Even the palette was imported from England!

Then I thought I was born to be a poet, get fame,
I found joy in putting words together creating rhyme;
It was a great feeling to see young girls cry
When I read those lines, which I called poetry!

My restlessness was still searching for an answer,
I was wondering whether it was literature
Or reproducing my imagination in a sculpture
And let go my emotions – sculpture was the answer!

But lo, life doesn't take the course you love to choose,
The least I dreamed of was engineering and science;
But that seemed to be my destiny, as it came to be
I cannot complain, science has been good to me!

I was nothing on my own, but surrounded by minds,
Bright intellectual minds dedicated to science;
Only I had to bring them together and create a bond
Like the thread that ties fragrant flowers in a garland!

Scientific miracles happen, when such minds try every day,
Science is made a tool to serve humanity in every way
Where nationality, color, race or religion can put no barrier,
We met, discussed, agreed and disagreed to reach the frontier!

When I take long flights with sleepless nights back towards home
I still think and wonder, just as I used to do all the time,
How nice it would be to throw a pebble in a still pond
And watch the ripples grow, reach the shore far beyond!

I also wonder how nice it would be just to watch the stars,
Twinkling endlessly, and the moon dancing among the clouds,
Telling myself, those were good years – we did something good
To humanity at large – though by some it is never understood!

To Sasha My Friend...

I met Dr. Alexander Starik (Sasha) in a science conference I co-sponsored and he organized more than a decade ago. We became good friends and met again several times in meetings. He recently bid his final farewell to all. I could not attend his funeral, but sent this poem which was read at his funeral service.

Words hide within your heart when it chokes,
The melody cannot be heard when the soul cries –
Cries for the loss of a friend, one of a kind, a legend,
Whose friendship I have cherished, but so soon to end.

Dear Sasha, where can I find that mesmerizing laughter,
Where can I feel that affection from a hand that is warmer?
It all look like a bad dream from which I was waken up
As I read again and again the message that shook me up.

It seems like yesterday that you greeted me in a land far away,
Several meetings followed, yet I was waiting for the day
To see you again, share the events in our lives in the yester year;
But now it can happen only in the thoughts of this dreamer.

Yes, I was blessed to have a friend, a scholar like you
And I am thankful for all those beautiful times with you;
I share the loss with your loved ones and our colleagues –
You have left behind a legacy that still clearly echoes.

Good by my friend, good by dear Alexander Starik,
We will feel your presence in the meetings as we speak,
We will hear your voice as an echo from our hearts
And your memory will live as long as science lives!

Section 4

Thoughts

Our thoughts have no boundaries. Sometimes we think about what is going to be or we want to happen in the future. But more often we get ourselves lost in the thoughts about the past – those precious moments lost in time and the wonderful events that to linger in our mind.

It's a Miracle…

I thought about those years
That have gone by,
But still linger
Gentle on my mind!
I thought about the times
I have carried you around'
I looked at the photographs
I took of you "my little girl"

And I wondered at the miracles
Of Mother Nature and time.
Combined they have turned you
Into a fountain of youth
And a beauty that inspires,
And gave you a spirit
Of understanding and care,
That none can surpass!

Like the autumn wind
That knows not its course.
I leave my thoughts
To drift across the oceans,

And I wonder
At the little girl
Grown – warm and beautiful,
Stretching out her hands for me!

And I still wonder
How I long to surrender
To the comfort and solace,
And the serenity and peace
Her arms can offer;
And cuddle as a child,
Seeking warmth so tender
As she did years ago.

Without You...

I close my eyes, try hard to sleep
    Or catch a dream to ease my mind,
But it seems, it is so hard to keep
    The feelings inside, and their demand!

It's not sleep I want, it's your love,
    It's not dream I want, but your warmth;
You are so far away, still under the same sky above,
    Near in my heart, so close still unable to touch!

It seems I am destined to think about you
    From a place so far away and so different,
I have to satisfy me by only talking to you,
    You may be away, but precious is this moment!

I wonder why I am here, couldn't get any sleep,
    Couldn't focus – a deep sigh comes from within,
A feeling of left alone, though with no promises to keep
    Yet tossed by own making, losing my own peace within.

Memories, Sweet Memories…

Memories, sweet memories that give me pain,
Memories, old memories of my days with you,
Memories, I long for to come back again!
I think of the songs, you so often sing,
Songs I wrote for you.
I think of the joys, you so often give,
Joys that I shared with you.
Oh! How fast the days have gone!
And you are in somebody else's arms,
And these lips of mine still spell your name!

There is a song, still unwritten, in my heart,
The song I'll sing for you, when you come back to me,
There is one tune for my guitar, I have never played
And I'll play it for you, when you sing with me;
Oh! How sweet is it to think of you,
And how difficult it is, without you near by me!
My days are filled with memories,
Memories, sweet memories that give me pain,
Memories, old memories of my days with you.
Memories sweet old memories…

A Fairy Princess...

There was music filling the length and breadth,
    Voices of folks singing loud filled the air;
Liquor passed through my veins, gave a warmth,
    But I was lost in thoughts about you dear!

I did not hear the voices or the music anymore,
    Those who danced vanished from my sight;
I turned, I could see only you everywhere,
    Your smile, and your laughter filled my night!

You were like a fairy princess, the fairest fairy,
    Carved out of the finest ivory by a master craftsman,
Dancing in front of me with the music in harmony;
    You were at my arms reach, only in my imagination!

Your eyes sparkled with a mysterious look,
    I could see the jealousy in the eyes of the girls
Who looked at you in the light shining from the back,
    Yes, you were so beautiful with those charming curves!

It's past fairy's time, you have to get some sleep,
    Can I kiss you good bye or can I hug you good bye?
May be someday, you will have memories to keep
    That I shared with you as sharing moments come by!

I Think of Thee…

I was sitting at the shore of Lake Tahoe. I had a note pad from Granlibakken Resort where I was staying, and I wrote this.

How often do I think of thee?
More often than those stars
Twinkling in the skies;
I stretch my hands to reach one of those
Knowing that I can't, just as I am trying
To stretch my hands and reach you.
Tune your ears to my heart beat
You will hear it spell your name,
Close your eyes and feel me
Touching, caressing and kissing you.
I am surrounded by young and old
Men and women coming
Out of the water so cold
With their hair drenched in water,
But with faces filled with laughter!

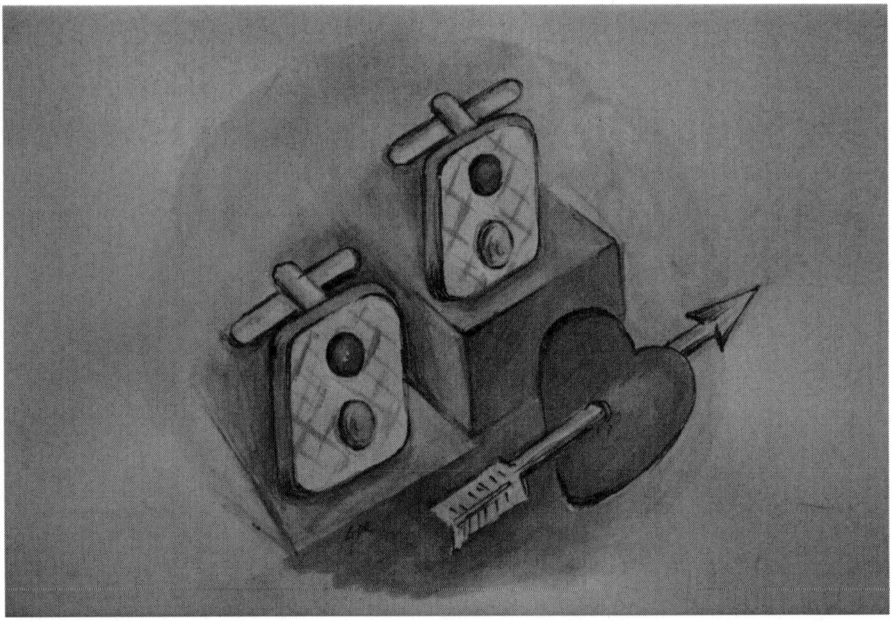

The Old Cuff Links…

I looked at the closet and picked the suit I like,
Took the shirt and chose the right tie to match;
But I noticed something is missing – the cuff link
They were there somewhere, but not at my reach!

Then I remembered the box of cuff links and tie clips,
She gave me on my birthday over four decades ago;
She didn't have any money, but still that was her wish
And she gave them in a box with a note and her logo.

A heart with an arrow, that's how she ends her letters,
But, that's not the only thing I saw in that small box;
I could see her immense love and care in each piece
When she picked those inlayed with ruby and onyx!

That box of cuff links will be here somewhere, I'm sure;
I spent hours searching each unopened box in the shelfs
And the drawers, shoe boxes and every nook and corner,
Thank God, I found it in a box where I kept old photos.

My heart was filled with old memories of sweet moments,
The tremble in her fingers when she put her arms around me,

And as she gave me her first kiss, I could see tears in her eyes,
Tears of joy, fulfilment and the happiness she found in me.

She had to leave me, destiny has its own path as we know,
I wish I know where she is now, and how she looks!
The country girl I knew, may be a grandmother now,
Every day, as I kneel, I remember her in my prayers.

I don't know how long I was holding that box in my hand,
It was like waking up from a long – awaited dream;
I looked at it again – our birth stones that came from the sand,
A gift expressing an endless love that ended as a dream.

Lost In Thoughts...

Sweetheart, it has been such a long-long time,
Seems like you might have forgotten my name;
But the very thought of you and your love
Brings an unknown serenity from above!

Have you been lately touched by the dry wind,
And by the hot summer nights that never end?
Have you felt the need to be together again,
Soak ourselves and drenched in our perspiration?

Last night, somehow, I could not sleep at all,
You were surrounding me in heart, mind and soul;
I could feel your bosom press hard against me
And I could feel your warmth penetrating me.

I thought it was a dream or my own imagination,
I tried to open my eyes with no change in situation.
You held me close, there was no chance to get away
Until I was lost in ecstasy that was here to stay!

Next moment, I saw you writing letters on the sand,
Your body still shining with marks of love left behind;
The moonlight exposed the divine and exquisite curves
Of your body-electricity surged again through my nerves!

There has been no end to loving in that hot starlit night;
And the sand made patterns on your skin so wet
As you rolled; you whispered into my ears, "I love you."
Everything was wonderful, beautiful, just like you!

Thoughts...

Did you call me last night,
Did you call me my love?
I wish I was there to tell you,
"I love you – very-very much!"

I wish I were beside you
To wipe those tear drops;
I know how much it hurts
When you hurt someone who loves you.

If the tears brought in your eyes
Are a measure of love,
Just remember I brought more tears
In your eyes than anybody else!

Am I a stranger, am I cruel?
A cruel stranger am I.
If cruelty is the outcome of love
Am I to blame when I have only loved you?

As the night waits for the dawn
And the dawn, for the rays of the rising sun,
I am waiting for you
My symphony and my song – today and always!

Need You Now...

She wrote back...

Are you sleeping, my love, did I wake you from your dreams
Or, are you tossing in your bed, restless to have me in your arms?
I could not control this heart of mine that wants you close to me
Now more than ever, I want to sleep by your side like a baby!

From the very first day I met you, you have somehow filled my heart,
I started to appreciate you, only to turn to a feeling that felt
    so right
Which filled me all over, touched all my senses, creating an ecstasy
That needed to be quenched by your touch, by your kiss, into
    a fantasy!

Now I feel lost, surrounded by an unknown universe, like a stranger,
Yet to sojourn, yet to explore, yet to understand, feeling lost forever.
But I see you with arms stretched, sleepy yet awake, dreaming
    yet see –
The look in your eyes, the desire they portray, and the unmistakable
    urgency.

I stop and stare at you, the soft light in the dark room,
> in a silhouette
Show your bare body I long to caress, I wish there is no end to
> this night.
Your lips part, you mourn in ecstasy longing to be touched, add that
> spice
Until we reached the sublime harmony where spoken words have no
> place!

Whispering Wind...

Oh! Whispering wind
Whisper not such a sad melody
For my heart is blue.
I wish I am free as you,
For all the freedom I have
Lets me make my own prison;
    Oh! Whispering wind
    Whisper not such a sad melody!

Oh! Evening breeze
Blow not so cold on my face
For my darling is not here
And I'm so far away from her,
I wish you could take me to the yonder shore
Where, I know, she is still waiting for me;
    Oh! Evening breeze
    Blow not so cold on my face!

Oh! Twinkling stars
Please don't laugh at my loneliness,
Wherever I am, I know she is mine,

Watch my breath, it still whispers her name.
I wish you could let us build our home
In your beautiful kingdom, so far above;
    Oh! Twinkling stars
    Please don't laugh at my loneliness!

Happy Birthday...

Have been thinking of you so much lately
And wondered how these years passed by;
Precious moments, and so much cherished they are
Preserved in my heart, in a secret corner,
Yet always stimulate me, fill me all over!

Be here, yes I wish you be here at once
In presence, not only in thoughts and dreams,
Reassuring that you always will care;
Time and time again, I want to hear,
Hear your heartbeat close in my ear!

Dear and loving and so needed you are
Always lingering and playing hide and seek, dear,
Yet too far away for the reach of my arms
To hold you, to caress you and fill you with kisses,
Otherwise those can happen only in dreams!

You be happy, filled with joy and laughter,
One that I love so much, and truly adore;
Under every line you will find, and so in all words
Only the sincerest, deepest and passionate wishes
Given to you by any one on any birthday of yours!

Random Thoughts and Unanswered Questions…

I wish I am free as a bird, I wish I could fly and sing while I fly,
And I don't have to find words for my songs.

I would kiss away those tear drops in your eyes
And taste the bitterness, rather than the sweet nectar of your lips.

How long this race for life goes on? Just a handful of years,
And what one takes with him or leaves behind are only memories;
Then why should there be sad memories?

What is truth? Truth is love and be loved.

If pleasure is the outcome of love, is pain the outcome of hate?
Why there is pain, even if you don't hate anybody?

If there be a Heaven, what will it be like?
If people who lived on earth are to inherit Heaven,
How can there be peace in Heaven?

Hell is burning fire; life is burning desire—desire to be loved;
If desire is worse than fire, hell should be better than life;
Then why is one afraid of hell if he can live on earth,
I wonder, nor do I find an answer.

If I cannot see my face which I can touch
How can I see my mind which I cannot touch?

Are the dew drops falling on the grass
A token of love of Mother nature or her tear drops?

I wonder how hate would be like;
If I know hate, maybe love cannot bring me pain.

Is love a bond of fetters or wings to fly higher and higher?

If I have given you happiness for years, and gave you pain for a moment,
How can I claim I love you?
When I say, "sorry" to you, I have failed in my love.

I have so many friends, if friendship is just a word;
But I have none to count, if friendship is unconditional giving and sharing.

To me friendship is love, a love without being possessed,
Where thoughts and desires are shared, but never claimed.

A love free as the skies, like the autumn wind, blowing down the valley,
Nobody to stop its course or race.
I wish laughter in our friendship and sharing of pleasures
With no guilt of indebtedness.

If I Could Read My Mind...

Am I trying to make memories
To last a lifetime?
Am I trying to make my dreams,
Dreams of a lifetime,
To come true in a handful of days,
Am I losing my mind?

I know not where my story began,
Many are the races I ran,
Few are the faces I remember,
Several are those I have forgotten;
I was foolish enough, at times
To yield to my minds insane thoughts!

There are times I have spoken
Words that were untrue
And found every rhyme
To undo the lack of reasoning;
Now I want to tell you

As plainly as I can,
How fast my heart is beating
And how I feel about you
And to be with you,
I know not how to find the right words.

Where Are the Words…

Yes, it is true; though my mind is full
Sometimes I don't find the words;
With a thousand fantasies.
I could not find the rhyme,
Words swallow words in confusion;
Thoughts lead only to delusion,
And with deep sighs, I close my eyes;
If only it will ease my pain.

   But now, I have found you
   All I have to do
   Is to think about you,
   Feel in my mind that loving touch,
   Hear in my ears, that sparkling laughter,
   Feel the look in your eyes reaching my heart!

Then, words come gushing through,
Words add to words to form the rhyme,
Generate music with gentle harmony!
My rusted imagination gets a new shine,

Like a perennial flow, all because of you;
Seems there is no end to my creation
Of the new combination of (unspoken) words
That add a brand new dimension!

    I have to pause, take a deep breath,
    Your thoughts surge through my veins,
    Create a tremor within me.
    Oh! How much I want you,
    How much I need you
    And need to be loved by you!

It Must Be You…

I love those love songs you want to hear,
    The melody and the words entice my heart.
As each day passes by, you become closer
    And so dear, I cannot get you apart!

With an aching heart had I departed,
    I still feel your presence close to me!
Yes, more than ever you I needed,
    I wish you have wings to fly to me.

Driving, I listened the songs dear to you,
    Tears screened my vision, sighs came from within;
Oh! How much I miss you, how much I need you!
    If need is golden, how rich could I've been!

You make me rich—rich in everything,
    I forget the heartaches that came along the way.
When I needed a shoulder while I'm falling,
    I hope your loving care, will keep me stay.

I try to close my eyes, get in my time machine,
    Remember the roads I had been through;
The time and places and faces forgotten,
    And those came to stay in my mind all the way.

If there was a life before this in which we live,
    I would have known you all the way through;
If there was someone I loved enough to believe,
    It must have been you, it must have been you!

Untitled 2…

Grass turning green
With the advent of spring
And trees getting new life
With leaves heaving in the wind –

Make me beckon
Life is a mystery –
Thoughts embedded deep
Wait a long long time
To find new meanings.

Though time flies
And the wounds heal
The scars never go –
The scars left by jealousy,
Hate and misunderstanding.

If the mind is clear
This life we have is dear,
It's for sharing joys –

Joys of giving
And understanding
Each other.

If I have only one life
I wish that life is for loving!

A Star to Catch…

Another demand, was it a promise made,
This artistic mind, of what it is made?
Imagination that defies reasoning
Or dreams that know not the beginning!

    A star yet to catch,
    A horizon yet to reach,
    A gift I cannot miss,
    A prayer that's still a wish.

Endless evenings spent in bountiful trance,
Blue skies, and the clouds' majestic entrance,
A canvas stretched, still blank on the easel
And precious moments I could not trade or sell.

    The colors, I have yet to mix,
    My restless heart, I have to fix,
    On the canvas, she'll always live,
    As in my heart, and joy she'll give!

Irony of Love…

A friend of mine had to leave his sweetheart and go back home to get married (for reasons beyond his control). He expressed what he felt and asked me to put those into words.

I know love gives pain,
I have heard, love is like a flower
That blooms only once;
But, why I fell in love again?

My heart beats fast
When I see your sweet face
And my mind is filled with joy
When you're close to me.

I feel like opening up my heart
To tell you something,
Which will hurt your feelings;
But some urge from within
Prevents me from doing so
For I can't bear you hurt!

Is my mind entangled
Or lost in agony?
Have I lost my all – my sanity
Or got lost in a lost world?
I try to be sober and realistic,
Not to live in a world of dreams,
Where life and love can be
As we wish them to be.

Deep sighs come from within
And your thoughts penetrate
Through the periphery of my heart.
As you said, my thoughts too
Drift across the miles –
Across the mighty Atlantic;
When I fly at six hundred miles
Towards my home,
My thoughts fly back
At six hundred times
Six hundred miles
Towards my love – you!

Sweet are those moments
I spent with you,
Like the nectar of rose distilled;
And to be close to you,
Giving and sharing, I felt
The true warmth of your love!
You are different
And distinct in everything,

You are a darling
I can be proud to love
And to be loved!
Yet, destiny is not in our hands.

Though I love you day and night,
Though I love you
In Fall and Winter
And in Spring and Summer,
Though you fill my heart
And the length and breadth
Of my dreams,
You cannot be mine,
I cannot be yours, always.
Is it not cruel to tell you
That I belong to someone else,
You do not know?

Season changes and days follow nights,
The tides rise and merge in harmony
With the rolling foam and the sand beside,
The trees wither to bloom again
And the wheels of time never stop.
The lakes and streams tell the stories past,
The moments of joy and the times of tears
Of loving hearts that met to depart!

Though I live in a yonder land
Sharing life with a girl you never met,
Though miles and miles of ocean

And mountains that rise high and tall
Stand in our way,
My heart will beat in harmony
With the sweet memories past,
Memories about you – my darling girl,
And I will love you and wish you
And pray for you life's best
Till my last breath is spent
And my earthly life is done.
And will you my darling
When you are filled with Heavenly blessings
Think of me – at least once –
Who once was so dear to you?

Still Thinking of You...

Filled with countless sweet thoughts about you,
Yonder in a country far away I still look for you;
Though mine and mine alone, always in my heart,
Yet at times hiding somewhere and so hard to get!

No spoken words can express fully and right
The serenity and purity of my inner most thought,
No matter how much I try, in vain, I can't refrain
The mesmerizing thoughts that will still remain –
    The thoughts about you!

Someday Soon...

Even imagining painting gives me an exhilarating feeling. But I wonder how swiftly these years passed by, and I didn't even touch my brushes. Like so many things one likes to do, longs to fulfil, dreams to realize, but never gets the time, nor the opportunity or the freedom, this too has been pushed for too long. In thoughts and imagination, one can achieve the ecstasy in moments, which may take years or may be more than a lifetime in reality.

Someday soon, I'm going stretch my old canvas,
Dust off my old easel and mix all the colors it takes;
Transfer my thoughts and dreams in yellow and crimson
From corner to corner, spanning the yonder horizon!
And as the gleaming rays of the setting sun above
Touch my body, and whisper the warmth that she can give,
Each stroke of my brush and each dab on my palette
Will give the forms unknown, a harmony I can relate
To the one she creates within me time and time again
And that's going to be a master piece – someday soon!

Watching You...

During my college days, a beautiful secretary joined our department. My friend had a crush on her and asked me to write some thing to show his feelings towards her!

You were sitting by my side
Lost, deep in the type writer beside,
I was watching you,
Admiring you!
Your fingers, with such a delicacy –
Seems like – carved out of the finest ivory
Played over the keys
Forming different words
That made no sense to me!
I wish if only you could type for me
The thoughts in my mind with that machine
That can never feel the human emotion!
I wish if only you could feel in your mind
The struggles in my mind,
If only you could feel
The dreams I want to become real,
If only you could feel someday
The way I feel about you today!

My Friend...

I often wonder and get lost at the clouds and the stars, the trees and the birds.
To me it appears that they all bear a message to mankind.

I looked at the dark blue skies
    And the splendor of the rainbow,
I saw a bird with broken wings
    Whose name I do not know
Singing, singing to me her songs,
    Words got short of my imagination,
But she can sing endless songs
    There is no need of words to her tune!

She fluttered her wings, telling me
    In her own way, she heard my words!
In vain, I tried to put words to please me,
    Seems, I forgot, music is above words.
I love the birds, I love the blue skies,
    I love the surging foaming waters,
The moon and the twinkling stars;
    And all God's wonderful creations!

I looked at the dark blue sky again,
    I saw the clouds waving their hands
Signaling, soon it's going to rain
    And I saw raindrops falling on the sands,
I can hear them say, as I waved good bye,
    'We are your good friends, we know you love us!'
From within me came deep sigh
    For I know I won't see again the same shapes.

Section 5

Family

All of us have moments of joy times of sorrow, troubled days when we needed a friend to talk to, to share your feelings rather than keeping them within your hearts. Sharing eases pain, provides a kind of relief which nothing else can offer. You, my readers have become my friends, and I am sharing moments of my life in these pages.

Abandoned...

Alone came I to this world,
There was no one by my side
To help me;
I was almost dead as my nurse said,
No one seem to be worried
About my life!

I was so insignificant
And I was thrown out on another bed
When they all worked hard
To save my mother;
Maybe it is providence,
Maybe it is God's will that I should live!

Then came nurse Thankam
To see this infant
Cold and blue as death could be
With no breath in his nostrils
And no movement of his body.
There did I lay, the abandoned child.

She screamed, was it anxiety or pity
In her voice, no one knew.
With her eyes sparkling
And her hands shaking,
She took the infant by his legs,
And spanked as hard as she can!

Nothing seemed to happen;
With her lips mumbling a prayer
And her face looking up to Heaven,
She raised him as high as she could
And slammed him against the mattress
On that lonely bed.

Some were shocked,
Others thought she was crazy;
But lo! She did the best she could do,
She did what she has learned,
Yes, she did the best she could do
In that brief moment in store!

God heard her cry,
Yes, He knew that she cared;
The little infant so blue,
Abandoned and lost for ever
Came back to this world
With his first cry!

Everyone around
Kissed nurse Thankam,
Hugged her and praised her

For what she had done,
Done what the doctors
Have failed to do!

One could see the gratitude
In that weak mother's face,
Having brought back to life
Her first born,
Who was almost left to die
A few moments before.

So, I was bound to live,
Live in this world;
And alone I came,
Alone I had to face this world;
But I used to stop and think
Of Thankam every now and then.

Seasons changed after seasons,
Trees withered to bloom again;
Years passed by, since then
I had my own shares of life's chores;
At times, I was tossed and torn apart,
But somehow, I made it through.

God has given me many Blessings,
Taken away some at times;
But then, I am always thankful to Him
For bringing me close
To those who cared and understood
This heart, let to die long ago.

Thinking of You Mom...

I remember the days when I packed my bags for the U.S. four decades ago. With no one that I know in the place I was going to and with $26 only in my wallet, it was an adventurous experience. Things have changed much for the better now. For the new arrivals from India, a number of friends and relative are awaiting here to receive them, and most of them come with a comfortable job offer. It was no so in those years. There were only a handful of Indians around, and there was no Malayalee (Keralite) in a 50 mile radius! The one thing that all of us experienced was home sickness. I missed my family and home, and my "God's Own Country." I found some solace in putting my thoughts in simple poetry. I found this one when I was arranging old files.

There is a brook beside my home
And the mango trees wave their branches
Over its waters.
It was my delight in my younger days
To climb up those trees
And jump into the brook;
Swimming across the waters,
I reach the farther shores

Where the black birds sing
And the plantain trees heave with their fruits.

It was my delight in summer days
To throw little pebbles into the waters
And watch the ripples
Merging in union with the shore.
I could hear the distant church bells ring
And see the golden sun set beyond the trees,
I could see the weary workers
Walking back home,
And watch the ploughman leading the cattle
Homeward bound.

It was my pleasure to watch the sun go down
And the glimmering landscape fade from sight
And oft an owl shriek from the tree
Announcing the dawn of night.
And I can hear my mom calling me home
Back to my sweet home.
I wish I am still a boy
All my life, watching the brook beside my home
And the endless patterns the ripple make
When I throw a pebble into the waters.

I wish I am still a boy
All my life, carefree
And unaware of this world's evils

Vanities and desires,
Jealousy and envy,
Worrying not about the morrow;
I wish I am a boy, all my life
With my loving mom's care.
My thoughts drift across the oceans
And reach the shores where they belong!

Dreamed of a Girl…

I dreamed of a girl – sweet, pretty and lovely,
    With eyes sparkling, dark and bright,
Her cheeks are soft like the petals of a lily,
    Like a plantain's stem, her body smooth and soft!

I dreamed of a girl, whose lips are sweet,
    Sweeter than the honey I have tasted yet;
Her walk, the loftiest that makes one to look at,
    Her beauty surpassing the words of a poet!

Her hands are like ivory, her lips are like ruby,
    Her hair dark and curly reaching her lovely waist;
Her breasts shapely, sumptuous and lovely
    And her walk like that of a fairy in the forest!

I dreamed of a girl wise and intelligent,
    Thoughtful and understanding, be my side
To give me inspiration, and to make this life prudent
    And adore me, care for me without pride!

Will never let me down whatever circumstances be,
    I dreamed of a girl like a comrade true
Who won't leave me, how foolish my actions may be
    And I found my dream girl when I found you!

God's Own Country...

It's the land where coconut palm trees
Sway in the peaceful air,
A land blessed with ocean on the west
And blue mountain on the east,
It's the land where art and culture
Are held to the heart so dear,
It's the land where education
Has been at the world's best!

I close my eyes, take a trip in time machine
To trace the past, my younger days;
I see the backwaters and catamarans
With fishermen on board,
And beautiful young women separating
The big catch from the rest
Blended in unison with nature;
Life seems to be so blessed by God.

I think of the winding roads
Along the hills that seem to have no end,
Feel the scent of fresh soil

Filling the air after hit by the first rain;
Hear the chanting from the mosque
And the church bells blissfully blend
In harmony with the music
That echoes from the temple, easing the pain.

People hold the name of their village
In esteem, respect the wisdom of the old,
Where "kathakali"* and "vilpattu"** add new value
And art always enlightens the soul.
It's the land that takes back to Parasuram,
And known as Kerala to the world,
But we call her, with love, "God's Own Country"
The blessed land of all!

---

*   A traditional dance performance
** A traditional musical performance

My Little Girl...

Losing your daughter is the hardest thing that can ever happen to you. I am unfortunate to go through this.

Pictures and memories
And a heart full of tears
That's all left behind,
I wish I'm gone and she stayed.

A rose that has just bloomed
Tossed mercilessly by the blowing wind,
I had to stay close and see her suffer,
Petal by petal watch her wither.

My life was wound around her
And now that she is gone forever,
I have no dream left behind to dream,
I wonder why I should carry on.

I had a daughter, I had a friend,
My worried heart, often she did mend.
With aching body, but with her mind so strong,
I did believe nothing will go wrong.

But the inevitable day came along,
She started her journey home, ending her song,
She was in a hurry, heaven-bound
Leaving me to cry, and peace couldn't be found

When I cry and am in deep sorrow,
My only companion is her shadow;
But when the world around me has turned dark
Even the shadow is so hard to seek.

I shed all my tears, my eyes are dry,
I don't even have the strength to cry.
With angels surrounding, she is in Heaven
And my every tear drop, she does listen!

Overlooking the mighty LA harbor
Her body sleeps in the deep shelter
And when I place a bouquet beside her
I hear her say, "Daddy please don't cry!"

I love you and miss you so much, my little girl – Daddy

Awaiting Surgery...

Thousands of miles away, my brother is awaiting surgery
    Hoping that life will be back to normal again,
And my sister-in-law is mourning her son's death - in misery,
    My wife, in our home far away, waiting for me all alone.

And here I am, a quarter of a mile below the ground
    Sipping vodka, lost in the loud music, may be lost my soul!
I look at the irony of my life, I know I am good in my mind;
    Maybe I'm like a kite in a young boy's hand, after all!

Let to be tossed by the gently blowing cold wind,
    I'm in the hands of destiny, like one seeking a rainbow
In a dark and dusty night with no light seen at the end,
    Yes, life has to go on, on its own path, like a flake of snow!

Her World…

Sometimes you take it for granted what you have. She is the best that ever happened in my life, but oftentimes I forget to say that. I wrote this on a Christmas eve with gratitude to the Heavenly Father.

There is a small corner in this wide world
    Where she seeks solace, pleasure and comfort;
It's her small kitchen, her own sweet world
    With her little fountain, bonsais and the rest!

She is a simple woman, never asked a thing,
    Never needed any, happy with what God has given,
Though life wasn't always as happy as spring,
    And tragedy struck her, as if deemed from Heaven.

I closed my eyes and look back on years passed by;
    That beautiful teen-age girl who stole my heart
And the times I tried hard, but in vain, just to say
    The words, "I love you", that got stuck in my throat!

The day came when she wrote back a letter,
    "Why am I so shy to say or gently whisper in her ear

Those words she likes so very much to hear?"
    Then I knew her love that has bloomed into a flower!

Time flies, years passed by, left their own imprints;
    Her tender fingers have wrinkles, the price of her toil;
Sadness often overshadowed her ever-smiling face,
    The burden is hard, hard enough to take away her smile.

But this is true, like old wine my love gets stronger,
    The words are there, which are seldom spoken;
As time passed by, we get older, but get closer,
    And there will be no end to love and passion.

Yet everything has a price to pay, love is no exception,
    Seemed like life has come to its end with no redemption
When misunderstanding blew up like hot volcano eruption,
    Making wounds, though heal, leaving scars to remain.

It's strange that I have taken for granted when she is near
    And miss her so much when my chores take me far apart.
I haven't often stopped a moment to say, "I love you", in her ear
    Although in my heart her name echoes with every beat!

Yes, I love her more than spoken words can say,
    She is still the same to me, that sweet teen-age girl;
Unreasonable, may be at times, but I love her my own way,
    The mother of my children, and to me, my all!

Back Home Again...

Written with thanks to the 'Flu, I had

    I'm sick and lonesome,
    This bed seems to me
    A prison of boredom,
    My mind sways far beyond reach!
    I close my eyes
    And I can see clearly
    The days passed by.

    I see the sidewalks
    I step most every day,
    The brook beside my home
    Where my dad taught me
    How to swim
    With her crystal waters
    Is before my eyes.
    I think of the endless evenings
    I spent, almost lost
    Looking at the horizon
    And the beauty
    Of the golden skies.
    The busy streets and movie houses,

Familiar folks and restaurants,
Ponds filled with water lilies –
All linger in my mind.

I think of John, my little cousin,
Who left this world so young
And the days we played together;
I think of Mary, our old maid
By the stove
And grandma calling
"Supper is ready."

I wonder how nice it can be
To be back home again
Leaving this land
Of green pastures,
Endless highways
And my new friends
To my country
Of warm sunshine
And coconut grooves,
Winding roads, sunny beaches
And familiar faces
And all my folks, sweet and dear;
Swim across the brook
Every morning
And watch the ripples grow.
Oh! How nice it would be
To be back home again,

But I tremble
At the very thought of leaving you
And I'm afraid
I may not see you again
Until I die.

Christmas from Far Away…

I have never been away from home and my family during Christmas. Now, here I am on the other side of the planet – I wish I could be there!

Christmas is a wonderful word,
It's a wonderful feeling,
It's a string that ties the family together
In a selfless and affectionate bond!

As I recall the sweet Christmases spent
In the sweet home of ours
And those wonderful moments of togetherness,
I feel that God gives me wings
To fly back home for the coming Christmas!
It makes me feel that sharing Christmas together
Is a bliss and real joy on this earth
And I will miss it all these years!

The hope that such wonderful days
Are not too far away keeps me satisfied
And fill me with sweet dreams and thoughts
About all my loved and dear ones!

These Christmas albums I send
Makes me feel I am there, sharing
Christmas with you all
Though thousands of miles stand on our way!

            Merry Christmas!

Still New...

I wrote this on a Valentine's Day to my wife.

After all these years,
    You are still new to me
And as a new day unfolds,
    Your face is right in front of me.

After all these years,
    Vivid and clear in my mind
Are those gentle whispers
    And the joy together we found.

Yes, after all these years,
    You are still new to me
And I love you all the more
    With a love always fresh and new!

Memories and Hope...

I am sitting here in my old sweet home,
    Looking at my mother, who seems so weak and lost;
Repeating her questions over a hundred time,
    Complaining she forgets the present, remembers only the past.

My uncle, once an eloquent orator lies still in his bed;
    He has a thousand things to say, I can see it in his eyes,
But his lips and tongue are locked, he cannot say a word.
    The once lively home is nothing but rooms of memories.

I turn my head, look at a rosewood bed tossed in a corner,
    The first baby bed I built for my sweet and lovely daughter,
Who has already left this world and gone further yonder.
    Memories sweet and sad are still lingering near.

I think of the folks of my own flesh and blood,
    With tears in my eyes, I reminiscence in my mind,
Who left this world to be with Him, both young and old;
    Stretch out and seek where peace and solace can be found.

I am filled with memories, thoughts fly faster than time machine:
    My infant daughter, like an angel lying beside my lovely wife;

The laughter she brought home and the joy to this heart of mine,
   The days of agony, the pain of her loss, my struggle to survive.

The evening my mother held me and my brother in her arms
   And told her friends, "These are my most valuable jewels,"
The day my uncle got me my first box of paints and brushes,
   And the days I have traveled with him in those smoky trains!

My father is gone, but I hear his footsteps in this house;
   This is not a home any more without his lively presence,
The things he cherished and touched are left here to lose;
   The more I think, the more I feel—life has lost its essence.

A question arises, should I complain, should I worry, should I cry,
   Feeling the unknown spirit consoling and guiding me through;
I have to carry on, there are still skies and miles to fly,
   And waters and oceans to cross, and my life to share with you.

New Year...

The beginning of a New Year
    Is the time to close our eyes, my dear
And bring to life vivid and clear
    Those precious memories of the past year;
Memories that have been blessed
    With the unity of heart and soul,
Memories that will surely withstand
    The tests of time that may prevail!

The very thought of falling in love
    Truly and dearly for the first time in life,
The very thought of being in love
    Truly and dearly for the first time in life,
The fresh scent of union still lingering,
    Still waiting for the unfinished conversation,
Still longing for the sweet whispering,
    All add new meaning and dimension.

When you are truly loved and needed,
    You are adored, and held in a pedestal

By the one you loved and so much needed,
    The joy that comes forth is clear like a crystal.
Every thought is s ray of light that adds brightness,
    Every breath is a feeling of being together,
Every moment is a moment of happiness
    Even though we are not physically together!

Though I need to be with you so much now,
    Though I feel the urge to hold you in my arms,
Though I long to hear the whisper of love
    And feel the ecstasy of your embrace,
I have to be contended that you are with me –
    In my heart, in my breath, and in my dreams.
Still I do long for the moment you be with me
    To share those things, which are uniquely yours!

My Valentine...

It's past midnight, it is dreamer's time,
My heart knows no reason or rhyme;
I wonder how I still have the sanity
In this world filled with mirages of reality!

The one I loved the most is gone
Beyond my sight, leaving me alone;
She could hear my cry, feel my heart's pain'
But now, my efforts to reach her are in vain.

The day will soon dawn, Valentine day,
A day I'll always remember, it's her birthday;
My Valentine baby is gone, yes gone forever,
In vain, I try to put the pieces of my life together.

Left in this world of jealousy and hypocrisy,
Where we are just taken as another commodity,
I have left love, affection, dreams and sentiments
For duty and responsibility, and to keep promises.

As the days pass by, I'm lost in this lost world,
But from Heaven above, like a flower unfolded,
She came again, asked me to write my song,
And though I can't see her read it, for her, it's my song!

How I Feel…

I looked at the pages of an old photo album;
Some pictures have faded away,
Like the dear ones I loved have faded away
From this world,
But not from my heart.

I could feel my anguish,
Tear drops trickle down my cheeks
And wet my lips;
Looked so strange to taste the bitterness
Of my own tear drops.

Yes, my loved ones are only in pictures
And in my thoughts;
They have left this world
On this unknown journey
To the place called Heaven.

Can I see them there one day,
Will I be worthy of that place,

I wonder!
Even if I can't be there,
I wish I could see them from a distance.

Sometimes I wonder,
Often lost and confused
At the very existence of ours!
What's real, what's dream
What is there, from here to eternity!

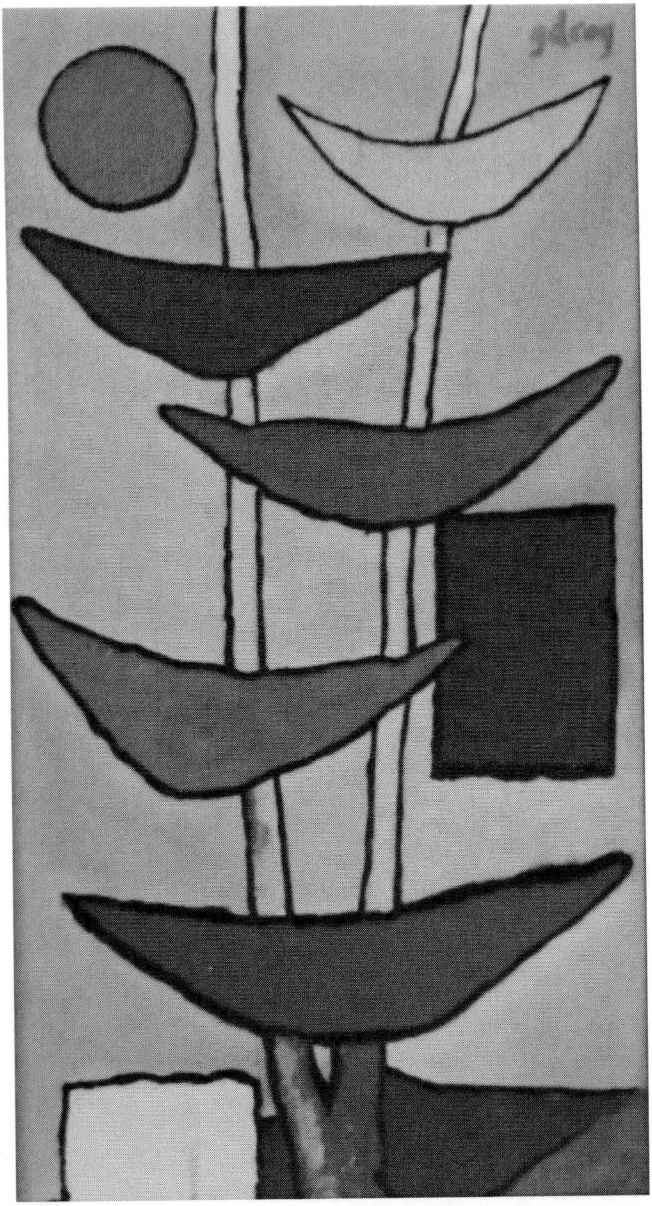

Thinking About My Home...

Cold blows the wind again
And the trees turned red divine,
Something in my heart whispers to me
It's a long time you're away from home.

The changing colors of the trees
And the freezing cold at the nights
Tell me that one year is already gone
And it's time to think of home, sweet home.

I have a home beside the gardens
Where my young feet tread over, all the seasons
And the memories of the sweet Christmases spent
Make me think of home, sweet home.

It was there I knew the warmth of mother's love
And the tender care that she bestows
It was there, I kissed my mother's belly,
Before I was born, that was my home!

Ours is a happy family of four,
A father, of whom, I'm always proud –
A scholar and the best teacher I have ever known
Who has never punished me, only loved me.

A mother whose love, I always cherish
Who taught me how love and humility can win
And a brother, whose wisdom I admire
Bold and daring, in contrast to me.

The wheels of time care not to stop,
They fly fast, leaving sweet memories behind;
We grow old with time, but our love
Like old wine, with time, stronger it grows.

I'm thinking of the sweet day of my life
When I can see my mom and dad again
And hug them with all the affection stored
To be back again with my happy family!

My Mother...

On my mother's gravestone

Lizzie Gabriel
(Mary Annie Elsie)

Hers was a life
Of love and purity,
Crowned with
Actions of charity.

A comforter for those
In any kind of need;
With a cheerful heart
She did always heed.

Give until it hurts,
She did she teach
Until the day
Did Heaven she reach.

Her life was blessed
For she loved those around,
The life she led, in our hearts
Will stand for ever.

Unknown Search...

I was so frustrated with little things gone wrong. Then my father's advice came to ease my pain.

The snowflakes try to cling to the trees
Only to be blown away by the chill wind,
Is Mother Nature too warm to melt this away
Or too cold to resist their unknown search!

Tress without leaves, like souls long forgotten
Show their dark skeletons on an empty sky,
The waters merge with the skies in the smoky horizon
That tries to put a screen between light and darkness.

I cheered up my soul with thoughts coming spring,
The shiny snowflakes seem to dance in the dark sky,
Looks like a pearl necklace on a velvet robe,
I wondered why I didn't see this beauty before!

I realized that most everything is in our mind's frame
As my father told me when I was very young,
That a half empty glass should be looked as half full glass
And that will make a sad one happy in any event!

So Much to Say...

I was troubled at this moment in my life. And it was my wife's birthday. I wrote this poem for her. My daughter-in-law read this in front of my family and was in tears when finished reading this.

I have so much to say, but I don't find the words
Though I have been good in finding the right words;
My heart is filled with thoughts, but I feel the emptiness;
I am surrounded, but I still feel the frightening loneliness.

I wish you could understand me, feel my heart's pain
I am not asking you, to try in any way, to ease my pain
But, at least, allow it to heal in its own pace of time
And stop pinching the wounds often, time to time.

You must understand, that I have tried my very best
To you and our children and will until I come to rest.
I might not have done all the things, all desires of your heart,
But I promise, I never ever even thought of getting you hurt.

Destiny has been cruel to us, we have shared the loss,
We have shared the pain, unable to find the words

To comfort each other, to ease the agony that grew within,
But God has helped us, you see, we are still "standing."

I think of the old times, times that so swiftly passed by
Those dear and sweet memories, in my heart forever to stay,
But, you think of all the difficult times brought by destiny
And dwell on them, always putting the blame on me.

Words came short when the mind is full, and so is mine,
How much you mean to me, spoken words cannot explain;
You close your eyes from seeing me and your ears from hearing me;
All I can say is that long gone are the life and spirit within me.

I see you still as the young girl, I fell in love with decades ago,
And I wish you, with all my love, a 'Happy Birthday' to you.
This is the first time and should be the last, to wish on this day
From an aching heart with pain penetrating the periphery.

Even after I am gone, I'll still be with you, can't leave you,
Close your eyes and ears, you will hear me whispering to you;
I will be around you to see you happy and to protect you
And my soul will wish many many happy birthdays to you.

Sick and Lonesome...

I am sick, but not lonesome, as I wrote on that day;
She was then at our home in a land that's so far away
And that day how much I wished she was by my side,
The beauty God created with His own hands as my bride.

Now, I am sick, but she is by my side comforting me,
Time flew so fast, decades went by so quickly;
She is a great grandmother, but to me she's still the girl
I gently kissed and caressed after our wedding bell.

I look back with gratitude how the Lord stretched her hands
To push me in time and saved me from falling down to pieces,
And from other dreadful accidents did He hold me safe,
Yes, God has been merciful to save me and extend my life.

Life comes in a mixed bag, yes, with joy and sorrow
And we often forget the love only He alone can bestow;
I have seen the extremes of both, and I see His mercy
In protecting this prodigal leaving home and gone astray.

To You Mother, From Miles Away...

Forgive me, mother, I was not there by your side
When you needed me the most and wanted;
I can't even be there to say that last good bye,
My eyes are dry, there are no more tears left to cry.

I have sweet memories of your love and care,
The times you comforted me, when the pain was hard to bear;
It seems that there was no moment that you wouldn't spare,
And you were always there to help those in despair.

You won't be there when I come home next time,
I can't see you come and unlock the door one more time,
I can't hear you tell the stories that stood the test of time;
Our lives deprived of your presence will never be the same.

But Amma, I can clearly hear you calling my name,
I feel your presence, hear your voice, it remains the same,
I see you standing by the door with a smile to say good-bye;
Now you have no more sorrow, no more pain, only joy.

Above all, you are with God surrounded by angels;
You will have a better life with Appa and your loved ones,
Who have gone there earlier to make room for you
For a life in perfect harmony; but we are lost without you.

One day by our Master's plan, I will see you in the rainbow,
In the clouds, as an angel with arms stretched to show
That your love endures forever, and gets stronger every day;
And I be worthy to be with you for eternity, this I pray.

                I miss you, I love you, Loving Son

Shattered Dreams...

I was a young boy, dreaming of the future,
    Dreaming of growing up, meeting the girl divine
Who will turn my life and dreams to nurture,
    Bearing children who can carry on what I left undone.

To me, art enlightens the soul, as only art can do –
    Dance, music, sculpture and painting one and all
Should be the breath of my children, just like they do
    Within me and create a paradise here for all.

Yes, dreams, one by one, became true, filled my life
    Just the way I imagined in my mind in my younger years.
Like an angel, a sculptor's master piece, she came to my life,
    Nurtured every bit of the artist in me, filled it with colors.

Sometimes I woke up at the middle of night, stretch my easel,
    Add a new canvas, start to paint, as she pats my shoulders;
She will mix the paints, wash the brushes – like an angel
    And as we hit the bed, the nights turn out to be such a bliss!

She gave me four wonderful children, each unique in a way,
    Blessing from God – beautiful, artistic and intelligent;

They could draw an apple when, 'A for apple did I say'
    Or an elephant before I finish saying, 'E for elephant!'

It was such a great sight to see all four riding their bikes
    In our nested neighborhood, and them everyone knows
And as they wave their hands to our neighbors, I could hear their
        voices
    In whisper, "God Bless you all" with love from their hearts.

There were paintings spread in the house and hanging on the walls,
    Music filled, with my daughter creating new tunes with her
        guitar,
With one son playing his flute and the other beating his drums
    And my oldest – daughter, singing seriously the lyrics I put
        together.

Wonderful were those years, with my daughter at high school
    Graduating at thirteen, winning the beauty contest,
        adored by all;
My son playing the drums in local parades and in his school,
    And as years passed by, all I dreamed along became real.

But God Almighty had His own plans, I could hardly understand,
    I had to stand by my daughter and watch her wither day by
        day,
Hear her last words, "Daddy, please don't cry" as she held my hand
    And then with tears, to hold her hands as her soul departed
        that day.

With no more tears left to cry, pain piercing the periphery of my heart,
    I held all within me, should I halt my life for the one who has gone
Or live with agony and take care of the ones left behind in my court
    Yes, God gave me the strength to live for my dear ones, and to carry on.

With my daughter gone, the music group came to a bitter strife,
    The guitar and the drums found their place in the garage;
My poetry came to an end, and so did my artist life.
    I was only counting years, time moved on with rage!

My children have their children, how time flew, I wonder!
    As my grandchildren grew, the old dream of mine came back;
There will be music in the house, the drums will thunder,
    Dancing will brighten our lives, yes, the old life will come back.

Seems like I still live in the past, grown in age but not in wisdom,
    Instead of Bharata natyam (dance), I see karate
Instead of drums and guitar, I see volley ball – changes with time,
    I am afraid even to tell my desires embedded in my heart.

When lighting strikes, who will care about the dark clouds,
    I had to see what I pray that no father would have to fight;
The world closing on my children leaving them in darkness,
    It's destiny perhaps that they gradually lose their sight.

I sometimes close my eyes, and feel how it would be like
    If you can't see this beautiful world He created to see,

But then, why this test to our faith, with prayers we humbly seek?
    At night, my heart aches, agony fills my mind, I cry within me.

If my departure from this world can bring peace and harmony,
    Cure all the problems, how could I be selfish and refuse?
But I have to live to help my children at times of need, when or any,
    Yes, I have to live for them with all my shattered dreams.

Remembering My Valentine...

I was in Boston, the city where my daughter left this world forever. It was Valentine's day, my daughter's birthday. With tears blocking my vision, I wrote the following:

It was Valentine's Day, and there she was with eyes wide open –
The most beautiful of God's creation my eyes have ever seen,
Like an infant angel she smiled at me, yes hard to believe!
My child, my daughter, greatest of God's gifts I could receive.

Years passed by, the joy she gave, written words cannot explain,
She was everything I dreamed of, everything I could imagine.
With the strokes of a brush, she gave new meaning to the canvas,
She gave a new life to a heap of clay with her nimble fingers.

She was my all, my love; I'll say, "the wind beneath my wings,"
The inspiration and the words and the melody of all my songs;
Seems like God loved her even more, He took her in His arms,
All I could do is cry and tear drops gushed over my cheeks.

Today is Valentine's Day, ironically, I am here in the city of Boston,
Where, on that day I held her hands and watch her go, never to return;

I am so sad, pain penetrates through my heart, I could not cry,
I have sobbed and cried so much within my heart, my eyes are dry.

Will I be worthy to see her again face to face with those hosts in
    Heaven,
Where she is an angel beloved of all, and my true guardian?
And when I close my eyes never to open again, will she hold me,
Will she remember her last words, "Daddy, please don't cry,"
    she told me?

I love you, I miss you my love – Daddy

My Father…

Written on his grave stone

A. Gabriel

His was a life
Of dedication,
Adorned with
Sincerity and affection.
An artist, a teacher,
A friend to so many,
His life was unique
In every way

His sojourn in this world
Was a full blossom.
Has enlightened many
With his wisdom,
And as he is gone
To Heaven, his home above,
In our hearts

He will always live.

"Weeping may endure for a night
But joy cometh in the morning"
Psalms 30:5

Just a While…

On the death of my brother's a few months old son

He was here just a while
To show us his sweet smile
When we wanted him around,
He was then Heaven bound.
His Father's call, he did beckon
Though it's hard for us to reckon.

The little angel that brightened our lives,
Now lives yonder with the Heavenly stars;
Just a little while, we will bear the pain
To see him in our Father's arms again.
Are you a distant star, our beloved son
Shining yonder in our Father's mansion?

His Mercy Never Fails...

My daughter was diagnosed with RP and she lost her vision in her early age. To see his vibrant daughter goes blind in front of his own eyes is the most difficult nightmare a father could go through, and I cannot control my tears as I type this.

My fingers tremble as I touch the letters in the key pad,
I look fine to those around, but inside of me I'm so sad;
I just opened the candy pack arranged by my daughter –
In what she did, she always brought me joy and laughter!

But if life is easy and full of joy as we dream each and every day,
We may forget God our creator and provider, along the way;
That's what it came to be in my life amidst bountiful blessings,
That phone call that changed my life, added more sufferings.

She had been good in everything she does, if she wanted to be,
Sports was no exception, and as favorite game tennis came to be.
We had so much fun, me and my four children in the tennis court
And she was the winner always, in each and every game or set!

Seasons followed seasons, years passed by like lightning in the sky,
She started life of her own, we moved on, she was not close by;

One day I was on my way from my home to Pennsylvania
And I got this phone call from her, and gone was my trip's
    nostalgia.

"Dad, I miss the ball as it gets closer to me, sometimes it hits me,
Am I going to become blind, I'm scared, please do come to me!"
I uttered all the consoling words that came to my mind to ease her,
Ease the fear she was going through, and to induce courage in her.

I do not remember the words I uttered, nor her words in reply,
But this I remember, remember what I did rather slowly.
I pulled my car to the curb, there was a stream that flowed,
I looked at that, the water made beautiful patterns as it moved

I closed my eyes, I could see those beautiful scenes no more,
How will it be, if this is the way it is going to be for evermore.
I thought about it, deep sighs came from within, and I sat there,
With eyes closed for hours, seeing only darkness everywhere.

If God answers all our prayers, we may take God for granted,
My prayer not to let her go blind or to take my eyes instead
Was not answered; His divine mercy He did show in another way
Gave her the wisdom and the strength to cope with it all the way.

Seasons followed seasons more rapidly, she is now mother of three,
Seems like years flew by even faster, and she came to be with me;
I thanked for God for letting me see all the things she could
    do so well,
With open eyes that vividly see, yet I could not do without spill!

I looked at the candy pack again, which she meticulously packed,
Tear drops started to trickle down my eyes, my cheeks got wetted.
With unheard voice I cried loud within myself, "Lord make her see,
See again the beautiful world You created for all your children to see."

How Fragile I Am…

I was watching a television show – a contest where students were helping teachers with answers to the questions for which they couldn't answer. Then came this girl on stage bringing back old memories. (29 October 2015)

How happy I was to watch this TV show
Where young students' intellect did glow,
Surpassing their teachers in the contest;
They did, row after row passed the test.

Then I saw this little girl, coming near
To help the teacher find the answer;
She was cute as my little daughter we lost
To destiny, God's will or to our own fate.

This little girl wore a golden chain;
Around her lovely neck, it did shine,
Twisted around by a thread made of silk
Just like I did adorn my daughter's neck.

Suddenly it brought back old memories,
I sighed and brushed my wife's neck, with tears

And let her know my thoughts about the chain,
She felt the same, which she told me with pain.

We lost our daughter whom we loved,
May be God loved her even more than we did
That He took her to His Home above,
Leaving us in this world, with sorrow and grief.

Section 6

Love

Love never ends, nor do we know the beginning of love. We can see the child's love the day he/she is born. We see God's love every day and night in various forms. Love is the most wonderful feeling whether it be giving or receiving.

Do You Remember the Day…

Do you remember the day, my sweet girl, when I said good bye?
It's like yesterday, and vivid and clear like the bright blue sky;
You were silent, you wouldn't talk, only hold my hands;
We saw so many good by hugs and kisses, and shaking hands,
But we only looked at each other's eyes, nay into the eyes
Trying to read the throbbing words that form in our minds.

I could see tear drops trickling down your velvet cheeks,
Cheeks that I caressed and kissed over a thousand times;
The tear drops fell into the coffee that's getting cold in front of you,
And mixed with it, as our very souls have mixed together long ago.
I wiped those tear drops from your cheeks with my trembling lips,
I could feel your body shake and tremble with your deep sighs.

"Main theri athar ka amrith nahin konch tha
Lekin theri aansuwom ka dhar pina chahtha,"
Yes, I didn't want to taste the nectar of your sweet lips,
But rather would drink and taste those sour tear drops.
My face was wet with your tears, as I walked to the plane,
And I was wondering, how I still remained sane!

Seasons changed, time and tide waited for no one,
The trees bloomed, withered and bloomed again,
And you belong to someone else, having children of your own.
Sometimes I dream and saddle up my time machine,
Fly back to you, to those quiet evenings, the starlit nights
And wonder, whether you too have the same thoughts!

Two Worlds...

She was just a little girl
Trying to get her mother's warmth;
A beautiful masterpiece
Of God's creation.
I was a teenager, looking for love,
Warmth and affection
And a loving touch and a caress.
I did not know her then;
I could not even stretch my mind
Nor in my imagination
Or dream she was there
And some day I will find her!

But destiny had its own way.
In different worlds we grew,
In different tongues we spoke.
Time never waits for mankind,
Seasons changed,
The trees withered to bloom again;
The little rose bud
Bloomed into a beautiful flower —

A sculpture carved with the purest ivory.
She was in my heart somewhere
Playing hide and seek,
Yet I could not relate her
To someone I have seen.
We both found our love on the way
In different worlds,
Still not knowing each other.

But something stronger was yet to happen,
Two worlds had to collide
In a harmony yet unknown —
To see and feel the love
That spoken words cannot describe;
To feel the ecstasy, to feel the magic
That is beyond imagination.
Life is blessed if one can see
The good in the other that came to be,
Giving and sharing,
Loving and bearing,
All that one can offer!

Above All…

I love to walk with you hand in hand,
    I love to hold you close to me now;
I love to reach and speak to your mind
    And see your face blush, and in ecstasy glow!

I love to lay my head upon your lap
    And read those mystic words your eyes portray;
I love to feel your breath, close my eyes and sleep,
    Rest my cheek in your warm teney.

I love to watch your lips part in ecstasy,
    Touch them, brush them and taste the nectar;
I love to be lost in your dreams, lost in fantasy
    And breathe in your ears, la amore, la amore!

I love to feel your intoxicating fragrance all over
    And merge in harmony with your heart beat;
I love to be with you now and for ever
    Until our hearts unite, and everything else is lost!

But, my dear girl, above all……
I love to be loved by you!

Want to Write…

I started to put words to my thoughts
About the various facets of life and fantasies,
Of human suffering – resulting from cruel mind
And the trials and triumphs of mankind.

I try to write about nature's ambience,
Its wonders and its real magnificence;
Of the frontiers explored and yet to explore,
Of man and nature in harmony and in war.

But honey, every time I try, all I could see
Is you with a smiling face coming in front of me
And all the words I try to put together
Turn out about you and your love dear!

Love…

To me, love is poetry
A spell-bound magic mystery!

Love reads like a fairy tale
But every moment of it is real.

The more often the word 'sorry' is heard
The less likely love is going to prevail!

Love is the keyhole
That lets you open the door to your heart.

When I see love in her eyes
I know I am in her heart!

Love is the bond
That unites the body, mind and soul.

People fight for love and die for love
But love never dies!

She asked me whether love sublimes,
I said, "No it evaporates!"

I was old and weak,
But love made me young and strong!

Gentle on my breast is my lover's touch,
Deeper in my heart, I can feel my passion build!

She was young, just begun to love
But she gave me twice the love I could ever ask for!

One is neither too old nor too young to love
If one knows what true love is all about.

Love is an addiction – once you are in it
You can't get out of it.

Love is all that I have
Love is all that I can give you!

I Asked…

I asked the autumn wind
That blows from the mountain
And keeps the golden leaves dancing,
What have you brought for me?
I kissed your sweetheart on my way
And bring her fragrance all the way,
On your face, to gently blow
And fresh for you, it will stay,
    Said the autumn wind!

I asked the lily of the valley
That spreads her petals loftily
And smiles at the radiant sun
What have you brought for me?
Your love is the prettiest girl,
I'll adorn her hair's golden curl
And when you kiss her in the dark
I'll twist my petals, tickle her neck,
    Said the lily of the valley!

I asked the cold rain drops
That fall on earth from Heaven
What do you have for me?
I have nothing for you,
But I'll make this world so cold
And your love will come and hold
You, as she feels my chillness on her face
For the warmth of your loving embrace,
    Said the rain drops!

I asked my dreaming mind
That is always trying to find
Where real happiness could be,
What do you really want?
I want my sweet darling by my side
And hug her, leave all my worries aside
And kiss her cherry lips,
Feel the warmth of her breasts,
    Says my dreaming mind!

God's Love…

If it hurts so much
When you stop loving me,
How much it will hurt God
When we stop loving Him
Who created us all?

When we ask for God's love,
He expects us to love others as well.

If you go to sleep loving God
You will wake up loving Him.
His love to you never fails.

If you love someone more
Than you love Him,
He may take that someone away
Because He wants you to love Him
More than anybody else.

God blessed me
More than I deserve;
His unending love to me
I need to preserve.

Thank God for giving us each other,
Thank God for the love we share.

As we hold our hand in hand
We pledge in our heart to dear God
That we will show our love always
As He has shown His love eternal.

Your love alone will suffice
When all around me despise.

Mystery Still Unfolded...

Palm trees sway near the ocean shore,
Wondered the same waters reach your shore,
If I speak to the waves, can you hear clearly
The message I send from my heart so dearly?

I looked at the waves, making endless patterns,
Never tired of romancing with the white and black sands!
I looked at the forms left behind as the wave recedes,
Only to be filled again by the wave that follows.

I think of our love that brought us together,
Everything is forgotten when we are together!
As we say goodbye, the marks of love are left behind
Until the next time we try to seek and find.

Your love is a mystic flower still unfolded
With its petals leaving nectar for hearts to be mended;
I look at the waves again and wonder at the mystery
That in their patterns, there is always a harmony!

What About Love…

Searching for love…

I searched for love Near and yonder;
Looks like the search was forever!
Then I found, to my surprise
I had only to stretch my arms
Because you were there,
Right in front of me vivid and clear.

Pushing love…

When one pushers one's own feeling
To extraordinary levels
Love tends to break in pieces;
Like a glass broken to pieces
It can be put together enduring pain,
But the scars will always remain!

Lost love…

How many times you told me
That you loved me,

But I turned a deaf ear
Pretended did not hear.
Now you are in someone else's arms
And here I am unable to bear the pain.

You Asked Me...

I could not refuse when she asked me to write poems for her, I did, I could see the gratitude in her eyes, which I can never forget.

You asked me to write more poems tonight
And here I am with pen in my hand trying to write,
But, your beautiful face comes in front of me,
I close my eyes and start thinking about you honey!

Do you want to hear what I really want to say,
I am a dreamer, what can you expect from me today?
I dream the impossible, impossible dreams about you
And pray, that someday they become true!

You are a beauty, I can spend nights and days
Just looking at you, watch every expression of your face,
Watch you tease, giggle, and feel your sweet embrace,
I have nothing to offer that you may wish.

When my heart takes control over my brain,
My thoughts, they reason only in vain;
I rather not waste this time to find out the truth,
But would write a poem that will tell the truth!

It's So Hard to Say Good-Bye...

With sorrow in my heart and tears screening my eyes,
I could see tear drops trickling down her rosy cheeks;
As I looked at her, from a distance, waving me good bye,
I could feel the pain in her heart, that reflected in her eye.

As for me, I could not find the rhyme or the words
To express the emotions that throbbed within my veins,
Glad I could be with her, and so sad I had to leave her;
I wished I could jump out, reach her and embrace her!

The distance between her and me increased though
And the roaring sound of the engines blasted through;
I was going away from her, not in mind, but in presence,
I tried to close my eyes, tried to be back in her arms.

Time and time again, I truly wished that I had stayed
Hoping that all flights are cancelled or delayed!
Wished I could be there looking at her lovely face,
And feel the love, the desire, and the passion in her eyes.

I knew it has been said, it is hard to say good-bye
And I knew it is difficult to leave someone, go far away,
But I knew not, nor realized that it will hurt so much
To say good-bye to someone you really love so much!

You Are...

Elusive...

How can I describe you,
    So elusive as you are,
Somehow, I think I have known you,
    Part of you here and there.
I want to know you completely,
As much as I hold you dearly!

Intriguing...

Sometimes you intrigue me,
    Raise my very curiosity
And I wonder what you think about me;
    Have I ever gotten out of my modesty?
Don't know the path of the cloud in the wind,
Nor the real thoughts that go through your mind!

Wonderful...

You look so wonderful
    Against the mist that surrounds you,

And you make me feel wonderful
    By simply being you!
As the sun comes the mist will fade away,
But my thoughts about you will never fade away!

Understanding…

I think you understand me
    Though I am a puzzle to many;
Strength to the often lonesome me
    Has been your company.
Though surrounded, I felt alone
I close my eyes, I am not alone!

Enticing…

Have you enticed me
    By that understanding smile?
In thoughts, though you surround me,
    I long to see that smile.
Thoughts about you are free to fly
In the vast and open blue sky!

Tempting…

You are so tempting
    And so are your words,
I wish there is no ending
    To the shower of your words!

Sharing is the blessing we have,
Without which, where will we be?

Alluring...

Are you alluring me,
    Is that the entrance to your heart?
Can I ever find me,
    Tangled, somewhere, within it?
My words, have they reached your heart?
Keep them there, as they came from my heart!

Lovely...

Lovely (person) is the word
    That describes you best;
When I'm lost in this world
    Somehow, I feel you I can trust.
Someone lovelier than you, I haven't met,
Though the real you, I have to find yet!

Delightful...

Delightful was (is) your presence,
    But time flew at the speed of stars!
Now, I'm lost by your absence,
    Why now time seem to fly at a slow pace?
I wish I could shoot a thousand pictures,
Captivate every inch of you that inspires!

Captivating…

So captivating are you,
    That my thought and my dream
Often surround you,
    Add to life a new mellow gleam.
Just a look at you, without words
Is often worth a million words!

Charming…

I prefer charm to beauty,
    God's each creation is beautiful;
To find charm isn't that easy
    And to feel charm is simply beautiful!
Should I call you my charming admirer
Or my delusive mind's mender?

Fascinating…

So fascinating you are,
    You created a new world for me
And so inspiring you are,
    You renewed the creativity in me!
So here I am starting to write again
The words so far, in my mind, hidden!

Poems after poems, and letters after letters, I wrote after I met her. A few decades later, met her again. Her voice remained the same – everything else has changed. Yes, destiny has been cruel to her, as it had been to me. As I retyped the above, tear drops trickled down my cheeks.

On Love…

One has to be in love
To write about love,
Love is not heart's imagination
But love is heart's realization.

Love is a feeling that defies age
Race, color or language.

You are close to my heart
Though we are so far apart;
My love is still so young and strong
Though I'm no longer strong and young!

To find the best
Was my true quest
I did succeed
In you indeed!

Love is a hunger that only love can satisfy
Love is a thirst that only love can quench!

I dreamed of a love that is soft as a snow flake,
I dreamed of a love that is hard as rock,
I dreamed of a love that is white and black,
But I stopped dreaming at your very first look!

When lovers meet after a long absence
Their spoken language is called silence.

If I say I love you only to please you,
I am cheating your heart;
If I say I love you only to have you,
I am breaking your heart;
But if I say I love you because I love you,
I'm giving you my heart!

Love is a wonderful feeling
You feel only when you are in love.

Sometimes love is like a kite
In a little boy's hands
Knows not the direction it takes!

Those who write songs of love
Derive pleasure and continue to write,
But those who truly fall in love
Are the ones who read what they wrote!

Then...

Spoken words had no meaning,
Except the silence, the look, the touch
And the ecstatic heartbeat.
But above all, the tears
That had so much meaning;
In a faithful gesture, they express
The feelings that are unbounded
In the heart.
Words can create magic
If they can reach one's heart;
Words can charm one's mind
If deeds that follow are true
As the words!

Then......

Words came gushing through
And words followed words to form rhythm,
Thoughts merged with thoughts in harony!
My words and deeds are true,
They follow my heart!

You Are, to Me...

Like a rainbow, you charm me with your colors,
Colors of beauty, charm, poise and tenderness;
Then you hide in another world far from me,
Reappearing, reassuring, you're there for me!

Spoken words cannot explain, how much I care,
Nor can they describe, how beautiful you are;
A sculptured beauty made of the finest ivory,
A combination of all I like in perfect harmony!

Where did you find the key that opens to my heart?
Where did you get that charm that can intoxicate
To the depths, where no one else reached before?
Feeling, dreaming, longing, hoping, yet still so far!

I like to talk to you, walk with you hand in hand,
And watch the foot prints we left behind on the sand;
I want to look again and again at your lovely face,
And imprint beautiful images that none can erase!

I wish a lot of things I cannot say or put in words,
But you feel them too, I have seen it in your eyes.
These simple words are true, "You mean a lot to me
And a lot more and a lot more as it came to be!"

Reason to Love…

There are things in life, easy as they may sound,
    But are so hard to reckon or explain,
And often it takes a truly special mind
    To understand what they really mean!

Often, they are unsaid and left by for thinking
    Or only cherished in the heart and soul,
For the longing, belonging and the sharing
    Are beyond spoken words to convey at all!

Like in a fairy tale in an old storybook
    We have to start when we are destined to be;
And all it takes is nothing but one penetrating look
    To start and roll along the wheels of destiny!

Is there a reason or rhyme, I beckon, to love?
    Is there an answer to the heart's deepest quest?
Is there a time or place to think or speak of love
    Or to make love, when two hearts really unite?

Even a stranded island will seem like a paradise,
    A crowded airport cannot break lovers' symphony;
All that matters is the time together in bliss,
    Together to cherish and grow in love and harmony!

More Aspects of Love…

Love's splendor…

Love has the splendor
Of the rainbow,
But unlike the rainbow
That loses its colors
When the light is gone,
Love gets stronger
Even after the spell
Is long gone.

Love to live…

You may say
That love is like salt
That adds taste to the food,
It is like the root
That brings life to the flower,
Or rays of light
That brings colors to the rainbow.

But I will say
That love is the air I breathe
And lets me live to love.

Mother's love...

My mother taught me only to love.
Sometimes I wish she taught me to hate.
How easy it would be to escape
When love starts to give you hurt.

Father's love...

I don't remember
That my father ever said,
"My son, I love you."
But I saw it every day
In everything he did for me
And felt it every time
He held my hands
With such a caring love.

Baby's love

I was looking at my baby beside me.
When her eyes met mine for the first time
Since she came to this world,
I could feel the depth of her love to me
In those speaking eyes!

Prodigal's love…

The more I go away from Him,
The more I love Him.
Some time I am so afraid
That He may stop loving me.
But then, how can He?
Though a prodigal, I am His son.

The Greatest Gift…

My mind goes through a melancholy drain
    If you are not there when I try to call;
I feel all my thoughts go in dismay and in vain
    Though I know your heart will hear my call!

I want to speak with you all through the night,
    I want to hear your voice and sing along,
I want to look at your beauty in the moonlight,
    And see the lovely patterns as you move along!

I want to whisper into your ears truthfully
    All those sweet words that lovers say
And see your bashful face blush so gracefully
    And that look of love in your eyes to stay!

I have seen all that I wanted and more, in you,
    The greatest gift I know is the gift of love
And the greatest gift I ever received is you,
    And all that you have given me in love!

Giving and Sharing...

My mind was searching
For one to share everything,
Body, soul and my all – I found you,
Everything I have belongs to you!
When someone likes my achievements,
You share my joys
And when my feet tremble
You hold me up by your love so humble!
Giving, getting and sharing
Life and love as one in being!

When your mind aches,
My heart aches,
When your face becomes pale
By the troubles that prevail
And when you sit – staring at blankness
In my heart, I feel an emptiness.
I feel thousands of thorns
Penetrate my very bones!
I like to console you from the pain
With words beyond human expression!
I wish I am by your side

To help keep worries aside
And forget the troubles that arise
To calmly work for a compromise
Of all the calamities that surround
And real peace of mind can be found!

A Corner In My Heart...

There is a corner in my heart
Where you wrote, "I love you,"
It gives rhythm to my heart's every beat
And so long as there is life in me,
    How can I forget you?

You don't have to worry
That someone else will take that corner
And rewrite what you have written
For no one in this world can be you,
    How can I forget you?

Your words will be in my heart
    Until I die.

And when I'm gone
And rest where I belong,
There will grow a cherry blossom
And a lonely bird will build its nest
On its branches
And sing endlessly in a sad melody
    "I love you!"

Why Didn't I...

Why didn't I talk about love
For such a long time, I wonder,
When every breath of mine echoed your name?
Why didn't I write about love
For such a long time, I wonder,
When every stroke of my finger spelt your name.?
Though words are neither spoken nor written,
My heart feels the warmth of your love.

"I love you"—how sweet are these words,
Sound melodious to a dreamer like me,
Who dreams the impossible dreams
And make them possible with you and me!

Remember the day our eyes met,
Remember the day our hands touched,
Remember the day our lips kissed,
Remember the day our hearts united,
Remember the day we were lost in our love
Only to be lost over and over again in love!

I was looking at the stars,
They did not twinkle yet;
I was looking at the skies,
There was no moon in sight
Because you are not with me!

Life's Blessed Moments…

Lately, I have been thinking of you
A lot, a lot more than your heart can imagine or dare,
Lately, I have been calling out your name
In my dreams, wake up, only to know you are not there!

This restless heart tries to find peace
In your sweet embrace, and gentle yet passionate whisper,
Wish to lay my head on your soft bosom
And close my eyes, as you gently and softly stroke my hair!

Though I desperately need you by my side
I shouldn't complain, destiny has been kind and good to us;
We had moments together, precious to remember,
We have shared a love that can even make nature so jealous!

We have waited years, for us to be together,
We pray for patience, and let's put our worries asunder;
Let time and distance nurture love to grow
That it will remain full in our hearts, be our hearts' mender!

Another prayer, my earnest request to my Master
Is to grant that my memory stays fresh and forever young
And as my journey comes towards its end – let me
Go away, with those memories staying fresh and young!

See In Me...

What do you see in me to love me dear,
    What do you find in me for you to surrender?
What do you sense in me for you to share
    Those secrets of a lifetime, held in a shelter?

A wandering, wearied traveler I was,
    So many missions and duties had I to perform
But my heart was searching in all places;
    The search was over when you stretched your arm.

Did you have the quiver in your body
    When our eyes met straight for the first time?
Did you feel that tremble in your body
    That told you something is going to happen?

I have had you since then in my heart,
    How long did it take to have you, doesn't matter;
You are fresh, vivid and new and so sweet
    As the touch of morning glow getting closer!

A World of Reality and Myth…

How can I speak about true love
Or write poems and songs about love
If I have hurt even in words once
The one who truly and deeply loves?

To me love is an endless dream,
An insatiable passion's stream,
A consuming fire from above
That can be quenched only by love!

Why do I ask you my dear every day,
"Do you love me the same way?"
Because it creates magic in my ears
When I hear, "I love you too," in a whisper!

I live in two different worlds on this earth,
A world of reality and one of myth!
A balance and control I try to seek
While tossed by promises as I speak.

Yes, saying good-bye gets harder every time
And I want you to be with me all the time;
When I say, "I'll miss you," and watch you go
I know it's my destiny I have to let you go!

Belonging to Each Other…

I want to feel your love, your tenderness,
Your care, your comfort…
When I say comfort, I close my eyes,
Think of that soothing comfort
That only you alone can give!

I feel like calling aloud your name,
Can you feel me, can you hear me?
Beloved, love is a wonderful feeling
Only in love, can two give to each other,
And never loose, always gain.

My heart is drunk with the wine of your lips,
Filled with the softness of your body;
Embraced with the tenderness of your caress,
Engulfed by the desire in your voice
Belonging to each other—how sweet it is!

Need Love...

Everybody needs love and be loved and the gentle touch of the beloved is the best of life's tender moment that will fill one's mind to its fullness!

I have been knocking
The door that leads to your heart,
You opened it with a smile,
Held me with trembling hands
And as I caressed them with mine
You felt the warmth I could give!

You showed me what love is like,
How sharing each other's emotions
Can create Heaven on this earth
How caring adds more meaning to life!

I look out, I see your eyes in the stars,
I hear your voice in the flowing waters,
And the splendor of your tender love

Could be felt in the breeze that blows!
Though you are there or close to me
In my heart, you are close and dear to me!

This World's Pressures…

This world's pressures push me hard,
    Sometimes beyond my own strength
And I fail to stop and say the word,
    "I love you," and make you know the truth.

But, my sweetheart, you have to remember
    That for every word that's unspoken
My heart has said it in sweet surrender
    More than a thousand times ten.

I feel weak at times, but have to carry on,
    Sometimes the load on me is hard to bear;
But I have to be content, and move on
    And count each day as a new song sweet to hear!

Lost World…

Is my mind entangled
Or lost in agony?
Have I lost my all – my sanity
Or got lost in a lost world?
I try to be sober and realistic,
Not to live in a world of dreams
Where love and life can be
As we want them to be!

Deep sighs come from within
And your thoughts penetrate
Into my heart,
My thoughts drift across the miles
And follow you!
And the more I try to forget you,
The more you fill my heart;
Isn't it insane that I love you,
And need you
And to be with you
When I know, you never said
'Yes' to me.

They say time can cure all agonies,
Agonies of love
And the disappointments too,
But what can I do?
I can't even count seconds
Without you!
I know life isn't so easy
As we humans think.
But I thought of telling you,
Now that you are far away
And that we could never meet again,
How I feel about you!

From Within...

You don't have to say you love me,
I can see it in your eyes,
You don't have to say that you care,
I can feel it in your caress!

But you don't know how much I'm tormented
Time and time again
By the events that have happened in my life,
That gave so much agony and pain.

These bursts of emotions keep me alive;
I'll be gone when these are gone!
It's no wonder I try to be at peace
With my feelings and emotions.

This heart was once filled with joy
And nothing but happiness,
But now, I live in my dreams, in a world
Filled only with memories.

Your love and tenderness have eased my pain,
I may be cold outside,
But you give me warmth from my very inside
And a will to survive and live.

Section 7

Passion

Is passion the outcome of love or just feelings of two people that cannot be explained? I have passion to paint, to write and one needs passion in love. It's a feeling hard to explain – I tried to put some words to it.

Lingers In My Mind...

She was sitting on a bench in that lonely park,
Lost, deep in the pages she read from the book
She was holding by her fair and lovely fingers!
The way she flipped – one by one – the pages,
    That posture still lingers in my mind!

I watched her, opened the sketch pad in my hand,
Started to draw her as if drawing pictures on the sand;
She noticed me, turned her body towards me,
With that enticing look that almost consumed me,
    That look still lingers in my mind!

She stayed still, her lovely bosom in my view,
I finished drawing her, had a feeling brand new;
She stretched her hands to see the drawing,
Asked me, "Am I this pretty or is it just your making?"
    That question still lingers in my mind!

When I said "good bye" to her, it was like the dawn
Of a new day – a new relationship was just born,

Handing a note, she said, "Call me over the phone!"
I felt her fingers gently and fondly caressing mine.
    That feeling still lingers in my mind!

I called her several times, but there was no answer,
My curiosity passed its limit, yes, I wanted to see her.
The phone bell rang, "Can you come to my home tonight?"
I wondered, asked myself – what's in store for my sight!
    That call still lingers in my mind!

She wanted me to paint her on a canvas – in full color
Not a pencil sketch like I did in my sketch pad before!
As I stretched my canvas on my easel, I was in for a surprise,
She was there as God created – no clothes – a masterpiece!
    That sight still lingers in my mind!

The painting was over, she was behind me, eyes focused
On the canvas and her image, and as she leaned forward
I could feel the pressure of her firm breasts on my back!
As I turned back, her perspiration my face did soak!
    That wet feeling still lingers in my mind!

I do not find the words to convey what followed next,
There was nothing between us, nothing to hold against;
We were drenched in ecstasy as our passion surged,
As pleasure beyond words was finally achieved!
    That pleasure still lingers in my mind!

Follow You...

The softness of your lovely breasts under my fingers
Sends a current through my veins that still lingers;
Fresh in me, is your body's unique intoxicating fragrance,
I wish I could immerse in it again, taste that essence!

My body's desire needs you, my mind's thoughts prevail
As if falling in love, truly with my heart and soul.
I could sense the feelings that still surge within you
That make me, time and time again, longing for you!

The sweet embrace, and the mixing of breath, mine and yours,
The harmony of the hearts and thoughts, unspoken words,
The comfort and the solace, the soothing touch – uniquely yours
All surround me day and night, and urge to follow you always!

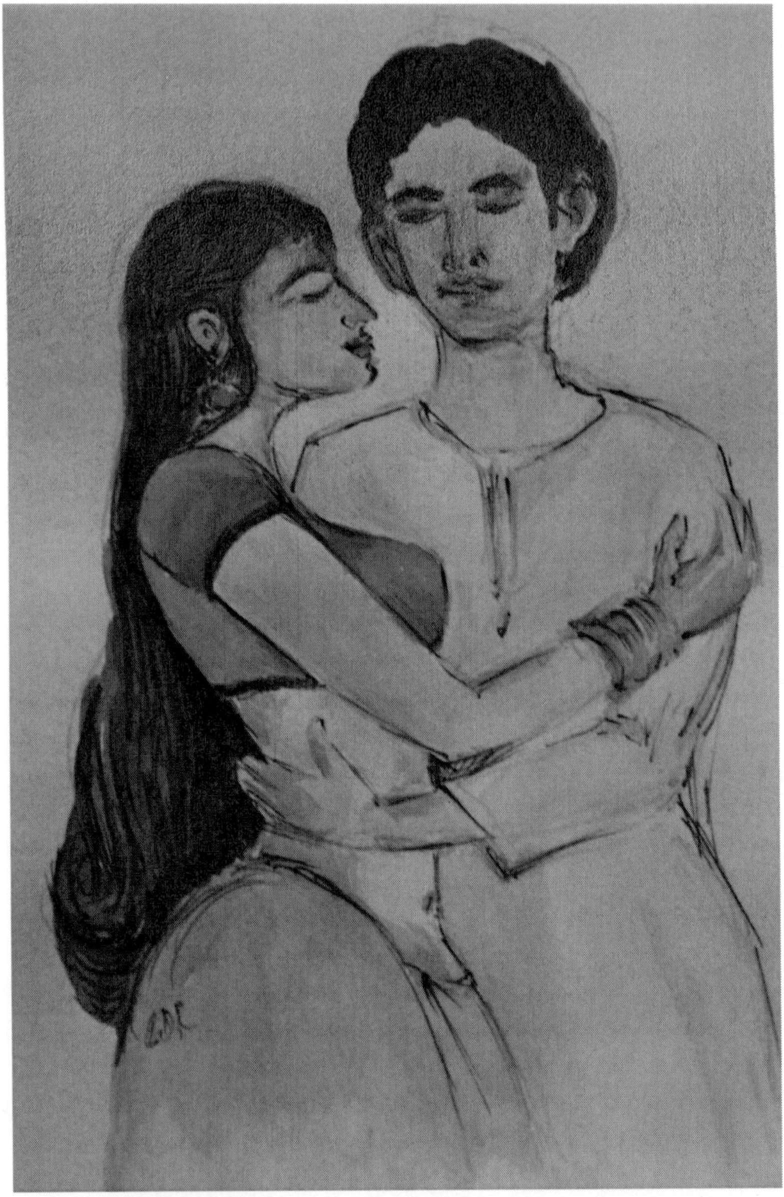

This Night...

> How sweet is this night
> With love warm and soft,
> My sweetheart, my dearest!

Love is a wonderful experience,
Warm as the sun's brilliance,
Cool as the moon's radiance,
Sweet as the rose's fragrance —
All blended into an ecstatic harmony;
What on earth can any other be
More wonderful than your love?
It's like rays of hope shining from above.

> How sweet is this night
> With love warm and soft,
> My sweetheart, my dearest!

Oh! How precious and dear is your love?
It's innocent, purer than a gentle dove.
Your fragrance intoxicates my senses,
I am drawn to you as my instinct urges!
Your touch touches my heart in and around,

Your kisses, like the nectar of rose distilled,
The sweetest, spiced with affection and love;
Intimate, an elixir for my life to survive!

   How sweet is this night
   With love warm and soft,
   My sweetheart, my dearest!

Your breast feels warm to my wet mouth,
That my songs get choked within my breath;
The only song I can sing again and again
Is that I love you, seems only the echoes remain!
Deep breaths come from within our hearts,
Ecstasy and rapture expressed in moans and sighs,
Sublimed with love—true love—above all,
Though 'my corner' in your heart is small!

   How sweet is this night
   Resting my face on your breast,
   My sweetheart, my dearest!

The warmth our bodies conduct vividly
Into our mind, heart and soul continually,
Added with affection, passion and desire
Drives us beyond world's limiting barrier.
I could feel your bosom heave and the longing,
I could feel your heights of rapture building;
I want to remain within you all through the night,
I wish the end to our loving is still out of sight!

Gabriel Delvis Roy

How sweet is this night
With love warm and sweet,
All night long, my sweetheart, dearest!

Rapture of the Cherry Blossom...

Like a velvet blanket spread with glistening pearls,
    The cherry blossom shone bright on that Monday morn;
Embedded beneath those late soft ivory snow flakes
    Were the pink flowers awaiting spring to sojourn.

Like a new born love drives a virgin to a heavenly glow,
    The early spring gave a mysterious blush to the trees;
The swaying branches giggled with a laughter slow and mellow
    And the breeze, though cool, set my body and mind at ease.

I closed my eyes, and the scenes I saw, time cannot erase.
    She was right there, tip toeing on the snow as a fairy;
I watched the snowflakes float and rest on her face,
    Intoxicating it smelled, mixed with her body chemistry!

Oh! How sweet it was to brush the snow with my lips!
    As my lips met hers, I could feel her body quiver;
Warm against my skin was the warmth of her deep sighs;
    She held me tight, I wished I could stand there forever!

Softly I bowed my face down to brush off the snowflakes
    That tried to hide away in her exquisite cleavage,

And as I buried my face between those lovely breasts,
    I could feel her heart beating fast and her bosom heave.

I don't recall what followed next under the cherry blossom,
    I could only remember her holding my hands and leading me.
One doesn't have to wait long to face young love's charm,
    It's there, one has to reach out and find that harmony!

Different Expressions...

Her reply – rewritten in poetry

Last night, did I become crazy,
    Did I lose my mind?
I know for sure, it isn't so easy
    To get you out of my mind!

But the more intensely I try,
    The more and close is your invasion;
In vain, I try to find out why,
    But honestly, it is like a delusion!

I listen to my favorite songs,
    They are your favorites as well;
You're the one who gave me those,
    And you fill my mind as well.

I read over and over again
    Your poems written only for me;
Teardrops fall from my eyes to my chin:
    You know what you have done to me?

May be this will be the last time
    I expose openly my feelings.
Can yours stand the test of time?
    Yes, I can read well between the lines!

My expressions are open, unlike yours,
    I'm afraid, the story isn't told totally;
But you are so good with your words,
    Only I can see what you mean really!

I would reconcile, have I taken part of you only,
    But I have taken more, more of your heart.
With your words and poetry, I feel happy,
    But a sense of guilt pierces my heart.

Our life and happiness come only last,
    We have too many bonds and obligations.
But then, I will be totally and completely lost
    Without you, and your care and loving words!

To Be With You…

Hey sweetheart, how are you,
    Did you have a good night's sleep?
Did you read my note that I sent you,
    Remember the promises we want to keep?

Did you see me in your dreams
    And let me wipe away those tear drops?
Did you turn to my side with a blushing face
    And feel the ecstasy caused by my fingertips?

Dear and near in heart, yet far away,
    I want to reach your sweet secret garden,
Where fountains flow and bushes sway
    To be blessed with your delightful union!

Enduring Love…

Oh! How sweet and wonderful it would be
To wake up and see you right in front of me,
Look at the lovely face smiling seductively
And those gentle fingers caressing me softly!

It's so nice to feel you stroke my hair,
To hear you whisper gently into my ear
The sweetest words I always love to hear,
"I love you very much," as it echoes in the air!

I long to feel your soft skin touching me
Everywhere, all over and around me,
I want your warm sweet lips pressing mine,
And taste the nectar and love all in one!

I wish to hug, nibble your lovely ears adorned in gold
And whisper to you stories that were never been told,
I long to be with you and make love to you
And be one with you, with nothing between me and you!

Dreams, as these may very well appear to you,
But honestly, from my heart I want to tell you
That you become fresh and new as each day passes,
And the more I love you with a love that endures!

Path to Passion…

Touch…

The gentle touch of her fingers
On my hands,
The gentle brush of my lips
On her ears,
The sweet whisper of nothing;
Words lost in words,
But pleasure unbound
For ever to stay!

Caress…

The gentle caress on her skin by my fingers,
A gentle squeeze on her soft lovely breasts,
A deep breath of her sweet lingering fragrance,
And the mixing of chemistry in perfect blends!
Spoken words broken at times, all lead
    towards
Longing, waiting, dreaming heart's desires!

Embrace…

Soft as snow, fragrant like jasmine
Her embrace intoxicates me,
Drives a surge of blood
Into every inch of my body!
A desire throbs from within
Palpitates the heart –
A desire to have, a desire to feel
And the thirst, yet to quench!

Lost In Your Love…

I was depressed, feeling lost deep in my mind,
Unknown fear and anxiety took hold of me.
And I was lost in time, in space and in form.
I tried to search and find the unknown.

The evening was dark and gloomy,
Raindrops covered my face, and chilled my very soul.
Muddy earth below, and cloud – covered skies above,
This earth seemed like a forgotten dream.

Though it takes long for the trees to change their color
And they wait long for the arrival of autumn,
It takes only little time, when there is harmony in spirits,
The clouds disappeared and descended a rainbow from Heaven.

I looked and looked, it was you clothed by the rainbow,
It was your face that brightened the dark skies.
I stretched my hands to reach you, and to hold you,
You slipped farther away, tiptoeing like a fairy queen!

Like the wave trying to merge in union with the shore,
Like the river trying to surrender to the ocean,
I followed you to the skies, smothered by your fragrance
And your sculptured beauty carved out by the Master's hands!

The rainbow was gone, you were clothed only by the wind,
God's masterpiece brought in perfect harmony,
A heavenly sculpture intoxicating my very senses!
As you held me by your hand, we left foot prints on the sand.

Time is lost when lovers unite, it was midnight.
The bashful moon hid behind the vanishing clouds,
Couldn't stand only blushed at your beauty and charm,
Lost in love, I tried to get close to your heart.

You whispered words into my ears, that are neither spoken nor heard,
I didn't try to find the meaning, I knew you cared,
Buried my face in the hallow of your lovely breasts,
I dreamed like a child, your fragrance mixed with my breath.

Our lips met, and breath mixed with breath in boundless ecstasy,
I could feel your bosom swell, heave against my chest
And we wished there is no end at all to this night.
Loving, longing, caring, sharing, feeling, we found!

Though Faraway…

It's a magic mystery, as it came to be,
    How your voice can create the magic,
That permeates all through and over me,
    That defies any reason, rhyme or logic.

Here I am far away, really so far away,
    Still feeling the warmth of your body;
I could feel your fingers gently play
    Unknown tunes that brings in ecstasy.

It's so wonderful to see you with eyes closed,
    Yet you know the right way to please me,
Each move of your body drives me so wild
    As you slid him in your slippery hideaway.

Words are seldom spoken as we move in harmony,
    As your sexy gentle moans reach their tempo,
You gently brush into my ears, "I love you,"
    I feel the explosion in ecstasy I can't undo.

And as you breathe heavily into my ears,
    Left with nothing to separate me from you,
Darling you offer me something new to entice
    And every time I feel how much more I need you.

Yes, what makes me glad, feel so lucky
    Is that your love towards me is true always;
Though we are near or so far away
    We are only at arm's reach, as we close our eyes!

Those Were the Years...

We were young and restless, filled with desires,
It didn't matter that you belonged to someone else.
You spoke the right words to touch my heart,
You had the magic to speed up each heartbeat.

I could not but surrender to your warm embrace,
My first man, but you took me with so much ease;
I was lost in your love, in your enchanting songs,
Those are melodies that stood the test of times!

We had our magic moments, moments of ecstasy,
Overwhelmed with the unique satisfaction of my fantasy;
You were gentle yet passionate, took me to another world
Until the time came along, and I belong to another indeed.

Years passed by, destiny took us apart in different directions;
My love remained, my need for you never seemed to cease,
Those stealthy moments we had were the only solace to endure –
Limited, being bound by society, tradition we so much care!

Yet, I needed you, needed your embrace and your intimacy,
I often tried to relive our past heaving moments of ecstasy!
It ought to be you, oh yes, it's true, I am not ashamed,
Know it is wrong, but do not feel guilty or betrayed.

I have to convince me each time, it's you and not him,
That's the only way I could be me, and please him;
If I see you now, those flames will burn within me again
Sorry, that's why I said "no" when I heard you over the phone!

On Your Lap, Like a Babe...

There was tranquility in the skies
And the loftiest music from the seas,
The golden gleam of the moonlight
Blessed the shore with the Master's touch!

But, in my mind a supreme solace prevailed,
I looked at the moon and the stars
And the unending patterns of the waves;
The moon vanished in communion with the clouds
And the stars twinkled when they made love.
The bashful moon can no longer stand
The frank sentiments the cloud uttered,
So, she came out, lighting the shore again!

I felt warm soft hands closing my eyes,
From behind, the sweet fragrance of jasmine
Blown to my face by the blowing wind;
I could feel the warmth of her bosom
Like roses that grow among the lilies

Pressing against my shoulder
And her nimble fingers stroke my hair.
I closed my eyes in ecstasy!

She gently led my head rest on her lap,
Continued to stroke my hair as if I'm her babe,
I watched her face when she leaned down;
With that lovely black mole on her rosy cheek,
I can say, my love, she is beautiful,
More beautiful than the most beautiful,
How pleasant and how fair is she, my angel!
Seems like all my drams came true.

I felt the taste of the sweetest honey
Of those cherry lips of her
While thy brushed intensely and teasingly
Against mine; I couldn't resist anymore!
I gently held her trembling body,
Cheek to cheek, dear and heart to heart;
With her breasts pressing against my chest
I could feel her heart beat, as two became one!

She wrote the word, 'love' with her forefinger
On my forehead while I slept as a babe on her lap!
I could feel warm sunshine brushing my face
And hear her voice, "wake up, it is morning already!"

Lost In You...

And she wrote back – rewritten

Can you imagine how much I miss you,
Do you know where my thoughts and feelings are?
Yes, they are tangled with you and you alone;
How could I return to my world
Since you changed my whole life around.
What shall I do? What do you have to say?
Over and over again, I think of those moments,
Those precious moments we spent together
And of the feelings, of the emotions, of the ecstasy
Which I feel, I have caused within you.
How long do they last, are they real
That last a lifetime, and more
Or mere dreams that pass by with time, I wonder!

Maybe it's easier to live life as it came to be
Knowing not those bursts of emotions,
That take you to a new world, a paradise;
But how terrible it would be, and what a great loss
For one to lose the capability to live to the fullest,
Give and get full love, share the sufferings,

Wipe one's tear drops, kiss them away
Taste the bitterness, just like the nectar of the lips.

Which is better, which is desirable,
What do I need,
I ponder inside to find an answer.
Maybe I want both, maybe I am afraid of both;
My heart trembles
In pain or ecstasy, I do not know!
My heart palpitates, is it the thought of you,
The thought of you touching me
Embracing me, loving me,
I wish I know why.
Maybe it's hard to explain,
May be there is no need to explain!

I have to openly throw myself into your arms,
I have no strength to refrain, your love is so strong!
How can I keep my feelings and desires from you
When I dream about them all day and all night long?
Should I be restraint, should I hide my feelings
Though my heart knows that I need you?
I need your loving touch, tender embrace
And your magic fingers all over me
Want your breath mix with mine,
Close my eyes and feel you all over – all night long!

Section 8

Pain

Pain is a feeling we all go through – I mean not the physical pain, but the pain of the heart, mind and soul. Whether it be a squirrel or a human being pain hurts. Though we may not be able to bear or share another one's pain, we can offer hope, companionship and pray for God's solace, comfort and peace.

The Song I Never Wrote…

There is a song in my mind, secretly kept,
The sweetest song I never ever wrote
And I will write it for you myself
On the happiest day of your life!

And though that will bear my agony
It will be filled with prayers for harmony
In the life that you will share tomorrow
With someone, whom I do not know!

For I hold as mine, your happiness,
And when you are filled with earthly bliss
And your life, filled with blessings of Cupid
I'll think of those happy days, that we shared!

If memories held dear can become real again
And if I have wings to carry me back again
To the times that so swiftly passed away,
How happy I could be in every way!

I'm kind of dumb myself to surrender
To human emotions, but I am no stronger

Than the bonds of true love and affection
And I dare not break them as a reaction!

For in my blood run memories past and old
And they mean so much to me, not to be sold!
They make what I am, especially for you to see,
If only for all day long you could be with me!

A ray of light passes through my closed eyes
That's you far away with your smiling face
I wonder where you are in this universe,
Maybe, safe in the arms of someone else!

There will be no ending to this love of mine,
I know not the day or where and how it began;
If there be another life after our days are done
And if God wants me, I'll be there with you again!

Do You Know How Much...

Do you know how much
    Your love means to me – hope you do!
Do you know how much
    I feel empty and lonely without you?

Like a bird with wounded wings,
    Painfully I was trying to fly above;
Just as she has no control on the direction she swings
    So am I tossed without your unending love.

Do you know how much
    Your words of love mean to me?
Do you know how much
    I long to hear you whisper those to me!

Like a musician lost his sound of music
    And his guitar lost its strings;
I was throbbing within to hear that music —
    That sound of your voice in my ears!

How can you think of depriving me
>   Of your love, of your touch, of your kiss?
How can you think of leaving me?
>   Look, but not touch, and not kiss!

I want you to keep me in your heart
>   When I'm away, far from you;
I want you to hold me to your heart
>   When I am close enough to feel you!

Longing for Happiness…

I had a real tough time during a few days. I sought out my feelings and words flowed into my mind as a gushing stream. I wanted to write it down, but I had no paper with me. So I waited for the airplane to land to write them down.

A thousand words came to my mind
    With reason and rhyme poured from my heart,
I thought I could write those down when I land,
    But now every word has faded away as my spirit!

There were times when I wrote about love and happiness,
    The joy she could give me being close to me;
Now the sunshine has turned into bitter darkness,
    What have I done to her or didn't to hate me?

Yes, there were moments of sharing affection
    And they are short lived like a rainbow in the sky,
What's left behind is a melancholy drain
    Like those left by the dark clouds that mar the sky!

I cannot find true meaning to my words,
   I cannot put what's in my mind on paper;
I am confused, don't know what are the odds
   For a happy life, once again to appear!

Lost In Your Thoughts...

You asked me, "Write me a poem."
I wrote, from my heart, my best poem
And I read it to you in that evening light.
Nothing else was there, in our sight!
You closed your eyes, and listened
To the poem, word by word till its end,
Which I wrote for you, in its entirety,
A poem of love written with sincerity.

The poems about love are sweet to hear,
But the pain love brings is hard to bear.
From within, emerged deep sighs,
The words brought tears in your eyes.
With trembling lips, I brushed them over;
And finally, the poem was also over.
I looked at you, your face was like an angel's,
Innocent, and true to your feelings.

You asked me, and I wrote again.
I knew what you love to hear and listen;
I wrote about the skies and the stars,

I wrote about the seas and the mountains,
And about the snow that clothes the earth
With white attire to its length and breadth.
Yes, nothing made me happier
Than to write about you, my dear!

So, I wrote about the beauty of yours
And your sculptured body that holds
The very nectar of life and love,
Which truly is a blessing from above.
I thought about your heart so understanding,
You were like a 'rose' with so much loving;
You showed sincerity and affection
That was in harmony and perfection.

You listened with radiance in your face
With gentle touch, whisper, and caress.
Time passed by; your kisses said you care,
Your embraces assured, you will be there
To give a helping hand when I fall,
To ease whatever pain that may befall.
You are like the lily of my dreams;
You whispered, you love my poems!

When destiny brought us for the first time,
I didn't want to ask even your name.
I know caring too much leads to hurt,
I didn't want to hurt you, nor to get hurt.
With every poem I wrote, we came nearer;
You took away more and more, and more

Of that corner of my heart that you filled,
I wonder how our dreams can be fulfilled!

You asked for poems written earlier in time,
I thought I will write my heart's rhythm –
My best poem, for you, I will write
Someday, when the time is right.
But you said so little, not even a lip's bite
For so much and so long I write.
Maybe I am confused, maybe I have lost you,
For reasons beyond me from your thoughts.

This is true, as the skies and clouds above,
I will never write a poem of love
To any one, because the pain it brings
Is more than the joy and the happiness;
We are all tied by so many fetters,
That are hard to break by written letters.
They make sense to a pragmatist's mind,
But never ever to a dreamer's mind!

That Old Picture...

That old picture brought memories of the past,
Memories of the warmth and care that I lost,
How can I complain when it's bound to be so,
There will be a time, when I had to let her go!

There is no reason or rhyme for that bond that came easy,
That united us together to a state of ecstasy,
My touches, my kisses are the ones she longed for,
Her warmth and her caress eased my pain, gave me more!

Sometimes passion knows not the boundary it has,
The body's needs defy reasoning or consequence that follows;
The comfort of the embrace, the solace of a gentle kiss
Can surpass all human endeavor to a heavenly bliss!

She is not mine, she never was, never could become one
And even the thought about wanting her is totally insane,
But do I have the control over my thoughts in any way,
How can I ignore those memories that are forever to stay?

Confused…

Thunders in the sky,
Clouds darker than death,
Gusty waters
Pouring from heaven above;
The muddy land below,
The streaks of lightning
Making wild patterns,
All add a mystic feeling
To this wearied heart of mine
That's so confused.

Have I lost my sanity?
Have I lost my reasoning?
Did I become a victim
To my heart's weakness?
The perfect road
Is winding beyond recognition,
Yesterday's sweet memory
Sounds as a melancholy tune
To her, I wonder why;
Life's a mystery, yet to solve.

But her's is a tender heart
Always to be loved and cherished,
Admired, not just within,
But spoken and expressed.
The ecstasy of passion
When quenched
Expects the solace and comfort
In the arms of her beloved
Until the dream is over;
I'm to blame for failing in this!

Feeling Like a Clown...

I feel like a clown, maybe that's all I am
    In this world of misadventure and exploitation!
I have been so simple, so naive, only I am at blame,
    May be someday I'll wake up and seek salvation.

There is too much deceit, too much treason,
    I wish my mother taught me how to hate,
Then I won't have this torture, this affliction!
    I gave so much love until it started to hurt!

I was a fool, I should have known from intuition
    That this life is one-way traffic at its best.
But the dreadful truth is there is joy in this pain,
    Yes, I have to carry on, there is no meaning in being lost!

If the Word 'Sorry' Makes Any Sense…

The doors are closing on my journey,
    But I have none to blame, nothing to say,
I have hurt all who have loved me
    In words, deeds, in every possible way.

It's so easy to destroy the castle
    That was built step by step on sand,
But can you forget, or is to possible
    To let go the memories behind

If I blame it on destiny, it will be untrue,
    If I blame it on my misfortune, I'll be untrue.
She gave me her body and mind, that's true,
    I blew my chance, only my pain will grow.

But my heart beats fast to tell it right,
    Though I have told this before, but failed to keep,
May be in another life; I will make it right
    If destiny blesses me to tell her before I sleep.

Looking for Words…

My heart is full of malady
    Filled with grief and pain,
Words were always a remedy
    To ease such pain.

But now, I'm looking for words
    I could hardly find them
And am looking for friends
    I could find none!

She used to hold my hands
    When they felt weak,
Comforted me with all her heart
    When she felt my pain.

Now I am a stranger
    In her thoughts and deeds
And all I need and desire
    Is her spell of love that mends!

Withering Away…

My days are withering away,
    Wasted days and wasted nights
Too often come along the way,
    My dreams are not close to my sights.

I lead a complex life, I would say
    Lost in a whirlpool of ambitions
That rock me and make me sway,
    Yet, I try my best to keep a balance

Times were great when you were with me
    But those too aren't easy to find,
I wonder do you often think of me
    As your face is always in my mind.

We had precious moments, just you and me
    I know you share my joy and sorrow too;
Your passion, your love made me brand new,
    Now, I'm lost without seeing you!

Tossed Between Reality and Myth...

Words kept unspoken die and wither
Like the petals of a beautiful flower.
As the petals crumble, tossed by the wind
And their existence is never left behind,
Unspoken words choke one's heart
Despite one may be a fool or very smart!

Words expressed and, by the heart received
Are like flowers whose nectar is distilled,
And preserved to spread their fragrance,
And kept for to reveal their own very essence.
But silence, like a virus can destroy the desires
And all those in life that one aspires.

Spoken words cannot fully explain
The pain that penetrates from within.
Reality (of life) seems often to give pain,
But a mind lost in the captivity of imagination
Can reach the yonder horizon of happiness;
But even if that be bound, nothing remains.

Sometimes, I need a friend to talk to,
At times a loving shoulder to lean on to,
Fingers that gently brush away my tears
And listening ears to melt away my sobs as whispers.
An understanding heart is so hard to find,
And even if one finds, it's so hard to befriend.

Dreams seems so much to please the mind
Let one leave, for the moment, the sorrows behind.
Tossed between the realities that can't be set apart
And the myths hidden in this dreaming heart,
Added to the multitudes of the day's toil that surround,
I wonder where I am really, truly bound!

If Only I Could Have Saved That Life…

I saw a squirrel leaping with joy
Across the highway.
I watched him as I came close,
I thought how happy his life is
With no regrets for the past
And no worries about the morrow,
Unlike my burning soul.
I know not what has passed through his mind;
He suddenly stopped and leaped back
Only to be hit without any mercy
By the front wheel
Of the killer, I was driving.

I know, I killed him
Though that wasn't my heart's intent;
Maybe my jealousy took his life.
There was agony in my heart
And I wondered,
Maybe he was leaping back

To get his loved one
To share his new trail,
Maybe he wanted to hug her
Or give her another kiss.

I can see his beloved
Waiting on the other side of the highway;
I have taken a life
And the love he can give.
If only I could have saved that life…

I thought of myself.
I'll be gone, may be soon, may be later.
I have promises that are fulfilled,
Dreams that came true;
But I have miles to go
Before my journey is done
And dreams, yet to realize.
But I'll have to live
After that day of journey into darkness.
I wish, I have another life
To do the things left undone.

Freedom In Bondage...

Searching for the answers
To a myriad of unanswered questions,
Setting to let someone free
Who never 'belonged' to me,
Could make one wonder
That I put my senses asunder.

Having lost in agony and pain
With only dreams left to remain,
I sometimes try to comprehend
What my mind wants to apprehend
A thought, a gesture, an unspoken word
May well satisfy my mind.

In bondage was I born,
And in bondage have I grown.
But can be love bound by chain?
Can reasoning ease the pain?
If trust abandoned brings hurt
What about love that defies trust?

Our conscience, rigid or soft it may be
Is not our making, it's made to be;
Only, we just follow it through!
A crumb is just not good enough,
And whatever the price may be
It's a quest as it happened to be.

I wish I had the words to say,
With ease of mind, I could convey
That one's value is one's asset
Which neither I nor Heaven can covet.
I wish my mind agrees to be so,
But now what am I going to do?

Some have the courage to fight,
Some are coward-enough to quit;
But I am torn in between,
My true world, have I ever seen?
May be as a dreamer I have to live
And as a dreamer, have I to die.

The Dark Side...

Old men
With cataracts in their eyes
Look through
Their thick glasses;
Frustrated women
With their drunken husbands
Shout with fury,
As their beer cans are tossed
By the wind!
Maple leaves
Get loose from the mother tree
Give a withered look to mother earth!

Is It Love...

I started to write a poem. Then I saw her walking towards me... What happened to my imagination?

You passed by my side in slow motion,
    Stroking me gently with your arms
Leaving the scent of your perspiration,
    That intoxicated my very own senses!

Do you really care for me? I wondered,
    Deep sighs of expectation came from within;
Though within me rays of hope gently gleamed,
    I should not make the same mistake again!

You came, sat by my side, we talked and talked,
    That gave me the strength I have been looking for,
A feeling of caring and sharing, in you I found
    And in the words, you uttered to this stranger!

I felt the warmth of your heaving breasts in my fingers,
    The fresh smell of your breath and the perfume
And the wetness of your lips – each still lingers
    And so are your words that you will be lonesome – without me!

But you never came again as you promised. I waited for you day after day until I found you sitting with another on the same bench!

Is the Soul Forgotten…

Destiny beckons, I could hear my Master's voice,
Scorching heat, sweating skin, and thirsty lips.
Nature's beauty, blinded by our own weakness
Where can I find harmony, solace to the mind in science?

   But where is art that enlightens the soul?

Mountains hidden by the misty clouds,
Winding highways that take you to the horizon;
Voices of people, moistened by the wine in their lips.
And the loneliness one feels, that echoes from within!

   But where is she, the one that brightens my soul?

Busy airports, crowded sidewalks, life goes on,
With research and reports, meetings and conferences!
People suffer, poverty, and painful deaths are going on
In increasing magnitude, what's the difference!

   But where is love that can reach each other's soul?

Troubled Times…

Oh! Lord, how I wish I have a friend
To open up my heart and cry,
There is no soul around,
Who could hear my plea,
Make some sense of what I say!
Have I grown – grown too old
That my thoughts are confused
And my reasoning failed?
Have I grown too weak
To listen to my conscience?
Am I victim, crushed and squeezed
With life's hard realities?

Words came like a gushing stream,
I could easily add color
And harmony to them
And create new meanings;
But now – thoughts embedded deep
Try to find new words,
But only suffocate inside
Nothing is clear, nothing is visible,

Only deep sighs come from within.
Where are the words gone,
Are they hiding,
Or have they disappeared?

They too, like my silent dreams
Failed me, when I needed them most.
Life is like a scary dream now,
I'm afraid to continue on
For the torture never stops,
And I am scared
To open up my eyes
Fearing, the dream may be real
I have made small mistakes,
I have failed in little things,
But now they all take monstrous shapes
And crush me from all around.

Like a creeper trying to cling on
To a twig burning at both ends,
I am trying to hold on
Between my dreams and realities

And they both try to consume me.
Life has taught me immensely
I have been through fire and pain
At times my heart bleeds and my soul failed
But somehow, I made it through

But now, my only hope
And friend at times forlorn,
Stabs me from behind!

Yes, my conscience is killing me,
This time I cannot make it through
On my own and on my strength
Unless You help me, dear God.

There Was a Time…

There was a time when she enjoyed what I wrote
    And my poems brought tear drops in her eyes,
But now, I am gone out even from her thought
    Yes, she needed me then to fulfil her desires!

I cannot complain that she drove me out of her mind,
    She was never mine, perhaps I didn't realize
That a day will come when my need for her will end
    And I will be the one and not her suffer the loss!

In sincerity will I die, since in sincerity was I born,
    I have never taken anything for granted, not love
To use it when we need and toss it when it's done,
    I wish she had been the same, when she showed me her love!

Tarnished Pages...

I look back at the pages of my life –
The crumbled tarnished pages
And those with bright colors,
I see the foolishness of my mind,
I see how I have played the game;
The only one game – the game of life
Did I fail, did I succeed,
Where am I in the hands of destiny?
Where am I in the path ahead?
I look at the times I was blinded,
The times I have taken a mirage
For real crystal-clear water;
The times I failed to see the real self
Of persons – being lost and carried away
By words that came from the surface!
The time I have lost in mistaking love
Or failed to share real and true love
Of those who became part of my life,
If mistakes can bury one
I am already buried into my grave!

Difficult Times…

No one knows the pain I am going through,
    No one sees how much I am hurt within;
Tears tickle down and often comes to rescue,
    Yet all fingers point out to me and me alone!

My shoulders are getting weaker to bear the burden,
    I could not find a moment for me – only for me!
I don't know how – with these hefty loads – I can carry on;
    The divine power that helped me through will stand by me!

Maybe, I shouldn't blame anyone, blame only me,
    I gave myself to my emotions, rather than to my brain,
Took pride in giving un conditionally, that brought me misery,
    All will end, when I'll be a memory, only to be forgotten.

Calm After Storm...

I feel the calm after the storm,
I don't know where it came from!
Maybe it's the healing rendered by time,
But still, though surrounded, I feel lonesome.

As before, this loneliness doesn't cause any pain,
I wonder, is my heart turned into a stone!
I'm driven to the edge, something I didn't ask for,
But what can I do, life isn't like as before.

I can still see the anger in her eyes,
The feeling of hatred in her very face;
She has two faces, the sweet and one with vengeance,
I can feel it even from such a long distance.

The harmony in our lives has been lost,
The love and caring are lost like a fading mist.
Why I'm to be blamed time and time again,
What the future holds is yet to be seen.

If you ask me, "Do you have peace of mind?"
I'll say, "No, it's all blown in the wind."
My body aches all over, but it's the pain within
My soul that I can't bear, with no place to sojourn.

My boat of life sails always in troubled waters,
All this time, there is the unpredictable turbulence.
But calm followed the storm, and I could prevail,
But now it's hurricane, with no way to avail.

Someday soon this will all end, will she then understand?
I doubt it, her heart is made of stone that won't bend;
I wish I could offer more, but my senses are lost
In the midst of all, I myself am totally lost!

What Have I Done…

Am I lost, have I lost my sanity, is my life entangled,
Am I drowning, with high waves surrounded?
In the web of hate, suspicion and mistrust
And you are pushing me in, instead of helping me out.

To hate me so much, what have I done to you?
Is your heart shut to all those I have done for you?
I have to write my feelings with the speed of sound
And look for the words that never could be found.

Why do you kill me so systematically,
Knowing that I love you unconditionally?
You have been cruel, forgot I too have a heart
And it's not made of steel to take this beat!

Can You Tell Me...

Can you tell me
Oh! autumn wind
Blowing down the valley,
Where is my girl, my love?
Whom I thought was mine!

Can you tell me
Oh! lovely daisies
Spreading your petals in the garden,
Where is my girl, my love?
Who doesn't love me anymore!

Can you tell me
Oh! raindrops from Heaven
That once shed blessings on us,
Where is my girl, my love?
Who has blown my castle to pieces!

Can you tell me
Oh! my weird and forlorn mind
That lost to feelings than reasoning,
Why you lament my girl, my love?
When you know, she is no longer yours!

If You Ask Me…

If you ask me, do you have peace of mind?
I'll say no, it's all blown in the wind!
My body aches all over, but it's the pain within
My soul that I can't bear with no place to sojourn.

My boat of life sails always in troubled waters,
All the time, there is this unpredictable turbulence;
But calm followed the storm, I could prevail
Though now it's hurricane with no way to avail!

Someday soon this will all end, will she then understand,
I doubt it, her heart is made of stone that will never mend;
I wish I could offer more, but my senses are lost
In the midst of all, I myself am totally lost!

Seems Like Yesterday...

It seems like yesterday
That so many things have passed,
It seems like, maybe tomorrow
Or maybe at my journey's end,
There will be no more sorrow
And I can give you no more hurt
And all these troubled days
Will only be memories!

Here I am next to you,
Still miles and miles
Seem to separate you from me;
Where is the love you used to give?
Am I that easy to forget!
All these broken dreams,
And all these broken memories
Still remain, though I lost them all.

Life is easy if you don't want to be loved
And if you need no one to hold on,
But I have broken pieces
Of love and affection

And clouds overshadow my memories' glow.
I am wandering round with no peace of mind,
No one knows my sorrow,
Do I have a tomorrow?

Section 9

Hope

No matter what the problems and frustrations we face, we can always hope that there will be joy and happiness on the way. Hope is what sustains us all!

True Peace…

At the time of your sorrow

The season changes, autumn approaches,
    And red and beautiful, turn the leaves,
Only to last a little time, the beauty vanishes;
    The leaves are thrown by the wind that blows.
Only memories remain as life on earth ends,
    And our dear ones start their journey to spend
Life eternal in a world in the yonder skies
    With the Father there, to sojourn in the end.

Pain penetrates the periphery of our hearts
    And sorrow chokes our very soul from within;
But by faith that gives strength in our hearts,
    One day, for sure, we will meet them again.
It's often said by all, "I share your sorrow."
    Unlike joy, sorrow has to heal from within,
And no one can share the other's sorrow,
    Save the trust in God that helps us to carry on.

Some say, time heals the wounds; but though
    The wound may heal, the scar still remains.

I know the pain you are going through,
    Because in my life, I had been there more than once;
I know how it feels losing someone you love,
    And the sadness that spoken words cannot say.
But I am sure, He who watches from above,
    He can give the peace and comfort when we pray.

His peace alone can mend our hearts' worry,
    His peace alone can ease our sorrow and pain
And He answers us when we are in dismay.
    Instead of saying I share your agony and pain,
From the bottom of my heart, I wish to say
    That I pray to God to give you peace and solace,
To ease your pain and console in His own way
    And restore this life's joy and happiness.

Wounded Bird...

On a note pad in Sheraton Pasadena hotel

I am a wounded bird, my wings are broken,
    Still I wish to soar up high and higher in the air!
I dream of the days when life was easily taken
    And the happy times, I thought will last forever!

Then the lightning struck, one pain followed the other,
    The rose garden became a brier of only thorns,
I even wonder how this cross I'll ever be able to bear,
    Only God's grace had led me through the troubled times.

Life seemed meaningless, not worthy to sojourn –
    Questions unanswered and prayers unheard,
But I didn't lose the hope on the One in Heaven
    Who still gave me the strength to move forward.

Sharing Your Pain...

More often you hear messages of pain from those you care. And you realize 'distance' is a sad word. You can't reach them nor find the right words to console them. She lost her husband, I lost my friend. How can I comfort her?

When the heart is full with joy or sorrow
Words come short, one has to borrow
And put together to convey the feelings;
I am in that state at the melancholy it brings.

It's hard to bear when someone you love so much
Is hurt so much, beyond spoken words' reach,
It will be untrue if I write I share your sorrow
Since sorrow like yours cannot be shared you know.

It will be untrue if I say time will ease the pain
Since I know time cannot ease this kind of pain,
Only it will teach you to live with it, live in emptiness
That is the reality that friends cannot help fully erase.

But this I like to say, I know the pain you're going through
For in my life, I experienced this, and still living it through;
He alone can ease your pain, I pray that this request He listens
That He stretches His hands and wipe your tear drops.

I wish I could be with you, hold you and console you
May be with the right words, add some solace to you.
But you know that my heart is doing that with every beat
That the next beat of your heart takes a grain of your pain out.

War for No Reason...

There are wars going on every day,
But a war is seldom taken seriously –
War between ideologies,
Politics and religion,
War between the rich and the poor,
War in the name of race and color
Forgetting the same red blood
Run in all humans' veins.

But don't forget, you owe mankind a debt
To fight the war against poverty,
Against discrimination and hypocrisy,
For freedom to live without prejudice
Believing in the family of brotherhood,
Uphold integrity, protect the abandoned,
Make this world as it was meant to be
By the creator who handed it over to you!

Out of Control…

Sometimes, it seems everything goes out of control,
    Am I a victim of my own thoughts, words or actions?
Does she know this finger pointing hurts my very soul?
    I can't bear the pain caused by unanswered questions.

The harmony of my life is shattered – one after the other
    Events added sorrow to my already mourning heart,
Often, I long to find and capture the right answer
    Whatever it may be, even if it brings me more hurt.

There is solace in leaving everything in Your Hands,
    A prodigal was I, wandering away time after time;
Stretch Your Hands, hold me and forgive all my sins
    And my thoughts and deeds are acceptable all the time.

Willing, but Forbidden...

Like a fairy from a yonder wonderland
She flew into my troubled life;
With her sparkling eyes and smile enchanting,
My broken heart, she did captivate!

My life beaten, time and time again
By the cruel hands of destiny and time
Found a new meaning I never knew;
Life is wonderful if one's freedom doesn't turn to fetters!

Love still is chained by the laws of mankind –
Willing to give, but forbidden to accept
Or willing to accept, but forbidden to give –
Love oft is tossed by the blowing wind!

A gentle whisper turned into soft-spoken love,
A gentle touch turned into a sweet caress,
And a deep breath expressed heart's desire,
A desire to live full a life often thought of giving up.

The Burning Candle...

Not only the clouds and the stars, the trees and the birds, almost everything that go unnoticed have a message to us, which we seldom realize. Even a burning candle has a lot to tell.

Simple things in life, make me wonder
And I often ask to myself,
Have I lost my sanity to be lost for hours
On matters so simple that pass unnoticed, most by all.

I have been looking for hours at the burning candle
And wondered whether she knows
That the life she gives to lighten the darkness
Can seldom brighten the darkness within the souls
Of many a people of today.
So, she sheds her tears, tears made of her blood
And with a mourning heart, continues her mission
Longing for a day (after her journey is done)
When all people will realize
That they are not made of leathern hearts to forget
That they owe mankind a debt –
A debt of love.

Like the blowing wind can end the mission
Of a burning candle and bring darkness around,
So does the cold hand of death
Takes mankind to a world unknown.
And like the candle, that's long forgotten
So are the memories of many,
Who in their times,
Have lightened this world.

Let's learn from the burning candle
That gives light with her selfless love,
Caring not for anything, but only giving
The most she can,
Caring not for herself, save others –
To look at others as people, as brothers
With the same blood flowing within
And stop the sorrows and pains of hatred,
Agonies and deaths of war
And the miseries and confusions of jealousy
And join hand in hand, to march toward one goal
Peace on earth……
Oh! How sweet it is for such a day to dawn!

Need Someone...

Though nothing around me has changed,
Here I am with aching heart and trembling hand
Write this note, without knowing in my mind
Whom to send this to, for I have no friend in need.

All whom I loved, cared and did the best at times
Of need, left me along the way in their own pursuit;
Yes, it is well-said, 'the good is oft interred with their bones!'
I need peace of mind, which I haven't found yet.

The one I have loved, held as my own always
Seldom understands me, I wonder how can she change!
And torment me most every day, with her words,
Words seems so harsh and hurtful to exchange.

I cannot blame anybody, maybe it's my own making,
Giving is better than receiving – the wrong philosophy
I followed early on, pretending as if I heard nothing
And let it continue until it is too late for recovery.

Reality and Myth

Life was blessed once beyond my own imagination,
Taken for granted all those bestowed in abundance;
Now it is time to think and respond to the situation
And catch the consolation seen only at a distance!

Real Freedom…

Freedom is a truly paradoxical word

If the freedom that you see around
Could keep you tight and bound,
If the freedom that you see around
Puts in prison your very mind,
Then what good is that freedom?

If the golden ring or golden thread
That adorns you, keeps you bound,
And your thoughts are put to sleep
And your dreams are buried deep,
Is there a real place for freedom?

In the world of one's own, I agree,
One is free as he or she wants to be;
But a world of two is infinitely blest,
Loving and sharing happiness at its best,
But how rarely there exists true freedom?

Don't Be Blue…

Please do not cry, my sweetheart,
Let not pain penetrate your heart;
I don't want to see those tear drops,
Trickling down your cheeks to your lips
For I am not with you now to brush your lips
And to kiss away those tear drops;
I wish I am there with you to embrace you
To ease your pain, take it away from you!

I could see you tossing in your bed
With so many words that are still unsaid;
I wish, Cupid blesses you with dreams,
Dreams that will take you to the skies,
To a fairyland, where only love is spoken,
Where you and I are left all alone
And rainbows shine all through the nights,
And the breeze intoxicates our spirits!

I hear the chirping of the birds,
Their music is beyond spoken words;
So is love, needs no words or speeches,

We can see it in our hearts and thoughts,
And as each of these thoughts unfolds,
A new day dawns, a new life unfolds,
With a new feeling, and a new meaning;
So, do not cry, do not be blue, my darling!

Easing My Pain…

Stretches of bright light in the sky
And the roaring thunder above
Beckon to me it's going to rain,
But it doesn't seem to ease my pain!

She is a princess, I am a pauper,
She loves reality, I am a dreamer;
But somehow, I met her along the way –
I wonder why she followed my way!

Seems it's true, love is blind,
Yet crazy as it may sound
I live in her heart as she in mine,
May be this is called love divine!

She doesn't belong to me, she never will,
Seems like it is destiny's will
That we should be bound by love's spell
Together we found harmony, I can tell!

Stretches of bright light in the sky
And the roaring thunder above
Beckon to me it's going to rain;
Seems to me, her thoughts can ease my pain!

Hard Times...

Words of consolation at the time of sorrow of a friend

I can feel your heart's sorrow,
Know how hard will be tomorrow
Because I too have gone through
The heartache that you are going through.

Know not whether to call it destiny,
No answer have I found by scrutiny;
Sooner or later, we all will be gone,
Life can be easier if we believe in Heaven.

Someday, I know, we will cry no more
And our hearts will heal from the scar,
But until then, these words I want to say
That peace of mind, may come your way.

Will You Forgive Me…

There is so much I have to share,
I need to tell you how much I care.
There is something I want you to be aware
That every moment with you is precious and rare.

Do you know, dear, how much I miss you?
Somehow, sometimes I do not know what to do
But the thought that your love for me is true
Gives me a strength that is fresh and new.

Honey, I am sorry that I have hurt you with my words,
Your every teardrop makes my love grow ten times!
Tell me, my beloved, where it hurts, let me ease your pain,
Foolish I was to hurt you, wiser I like to remain.

How often I think of the day you came into my life
And that look in your eyes that changed my life;
Dreams they may seem, but often came to be true,
The more I know you, the more I love to be with you.

Turn to me, my beloved, let me wipe those tear drops,
Lay beside me, let me comfort you with the right words!
Will you forgive me if I say a hundred words to console
For every word that hurts you; I love you in heart and soul!

Those Memories…

Memories that never die,
Memories that bring a deep sigh
Memories that mixed with my blood
Are the memories of you!

It was heavenly sunshine,
Moonlit nights and starry skies
And you my loving darling, by my side
With the rippling waters echoing our song
And the twinkling of the lightning bugs
And the whispering of the evening breeze,
Oh! How sweet were those moments!
I feel I live by those memories.

You are still with me, and all we do
Help us store more and more memories,
So, let us start gathering, memories we can –
All the sweet memories we can
For a day may come
When we can't gather memories any more.

Then all the memories we gathered
In the short time we were together
Will keep us together
For a lifetime if only in our minds
And if there be a world after death
I'm sure, we will share our lives together
All our times.

You Are the One…

I find new strength in adversity
    When you caringly stand by me;
My thoughts are covered with purity
    When you gently caress me!

I become a brand new person
    When you lovingly embrace me;
I feel the ecstasy so far unknown
    When you start kissing me!

This life, how difficult it may be,
    Turns into a paradise with sunshine,
When nothing separates you and me,
    When we are one, the only one!

You are the one who came to share
Your life with me.

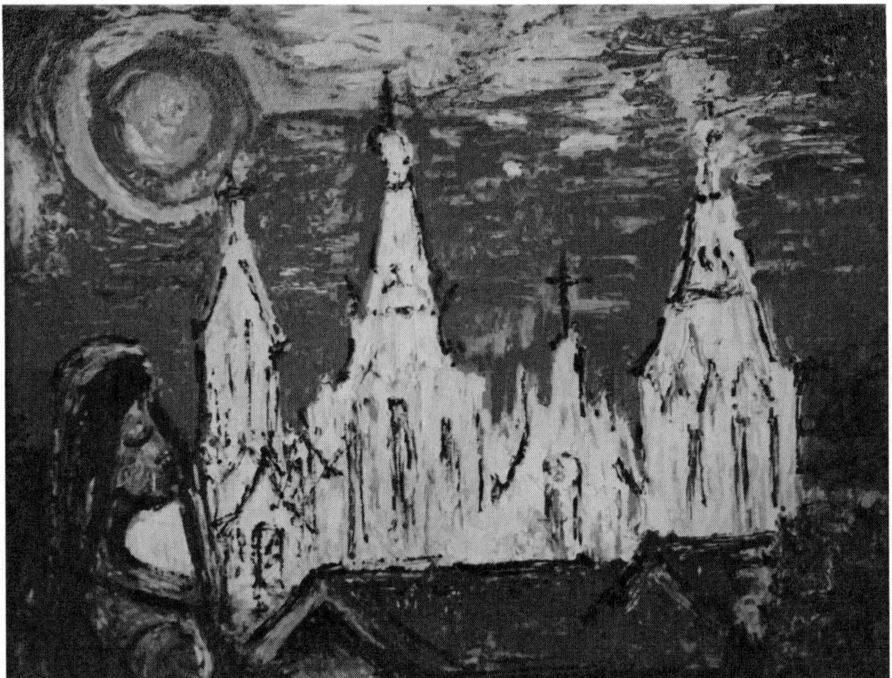

Her Prayer Will Be Heard…

The melodious sound of the church bells filled the air,
    Yonder I saw the church built with magnificent beauty;
The white steeples reached the skies, looked even higher,
    I could feel the presence of God in the glorious sanctuary.

I saw a woman outside the church, kneeling and beating repeatedly
    Her breasts with both hands, sobbing filled with tears;
I know not why she cried, worrying not about those passing by,
    I could see her pain, it was so clearly written on her face.

Did she lose somebody very dear to her to the hands of destiny,
    Did she lose all she had by the cruel act of some body?
It has become so common that we see so many forms of tragedy,
    Poor and helpless folks exploited by the powerful, led to poverty.

The more I looked at her, I felt those were not tears of sorrow,
    But that of repentance of something she did and regretted,
Maybe, she sold her body to have an easy life, I do not know;
    But this I know, my heart tells me so, her prayer will be heard!

A Little Rose Bud…

A little rose bud,
Like an angel from Heaven
Flew into my arms
And as I watched
It bloomed into a flower
With all the fragrance known;
Now that flower adorns my heart
And fills me with warmth and love.

I don't want to part that flower,
I can't bear someone taste its nectar,
But if it can adorn a place
Better than my heart,
Soon, I have to let it go;
For the flower has only blossomed
And I have no right
To keep it all my own.

In My Heart...

Have I told you lately
  That I adore you?
Did I whisper softly
  That I love you?

If your silence means, I do
  How glad I would be!
And if silence is gold,
  How rich I would be!

But your unspoken words
  Are worth a thousand songs.
If distance is the saddest of all words,
  All I need (to fly to you) are wings!

I still remember your first look
  And those eyes that can penetrate;
But seldom did I, then think
  That you will remain in my heart!

I sometimes wonder
>How two strangers can meet,

Clearly and vividly remember
>Every single moment together spent.

It's true, it's a good feeling
>That you do really care.

But sometimes hearing is believing,
>Hence, these questions I venture!

But your eyes have spoken well
>And I can read it in your face,

That bond of a divine spell,
>That time and distance cannot erase!

Wearied Moments...

It's so real, it's there,
My heart knows;
The desires and dreams,
I can see them, they are there,
And I try,
But I can't reach them!

I could feel the window pane
That won't let me reach,
I could feel the passion
But won't let me touch;
I see her lips move,
But I can't hear her voice!

Man's leathern heart
Made rules to defy love;
Woman's jealousy
Weaves unwanted barrier
To put love asunder;
But true love conquers all!

Turbulent Waters...

My ship sails in cold and turbulent waters,
    Sometime there appears a brief calm
But then everything, in a few moments, changes
    And what follows is a deadly storm!

I wonder how long I can carry on
    Fighting the raging waters and their motion;
I only think of the good times long gone,
    Try to forget the thought of what can happen.

Then I see beyond the hazy horizon,
    There is a shore truly bright and green
And the waving hands of a sweet loving person
    Beckoning, "I'm waiting for you, come on!"

Yes, difficulties may come in one's way,
    But there will be calm after storm;
Nothing can stand between nor make me sway,
    I will be with you to share true love's blossom!

I'll Make It Up With You...

I'm finding moonlight in perfect darkness,
Finding a haven for shelter amidst torrid waters,
Finding new order to change the chains of events
When I try to close my eyes and see your face!

'Sorry' is not a word good enough to make up
For all the pain and frustration, I have added up.
But I can assure you, and you know it too
That I will make it up the next time I'm with you!

You Are...

Simply the very best,
    The best words only can explain
How much I am blest
    To have you for me to sojourn!

Beaten and shaken for long
    So much, I could not refrain;
But somehow you came along
    Giving me strength to sustain.

Thoughts about you,
    Reassure me, help me maintain
My creativity and poetry,
    Add meaning, to words they contain!

Are You Drifting Away…

Why do we sit like strangers,
    Close to each other, yet in worlds apart;
Caught up in the web of circumstances,
    Only to bring pain and hurt?

Why is this heavy window pane
    Between you and me my dear;
Seeing, yet trying to hide within
    Our feelings, though sincere and pure?

I'm glad you're engraved in my heart
    And nothing could erase it away;
Neither time, nor the wavering of your heart
    Can play any role, you are here to stay!

Beyond Words…

Day to day problems make me sick,
But your thoughtful words have the trick
To cheer me up, so my pain would be gone
And to remind me that lot is left to be done.

I need a private room for me in my life
And spend some time without any strife
To do things I enjoy and think do well,
And to be lost in a sweet and splendid spell.

Yes, life has been tough, and somehow,
Right or wrong, I have made it through;
Though like the glow of the rainbow in the sky
Some of my dreams have faded away.

I still long for a journey in this world
With understanding and resolve so bold
That true happiness will be on my way
Beyond the words I have learned can say.

Life's Precious Moments...

Life's precious moments,
    Embedded like a rose
Amidst pricking thorns,
    Are difficult at times
To stretch out and reach!
    But the happiness they give
Endures, and enlightens so much,
    That it's possible to survive
The trials that make us dismay,
    And the pain that makes us cry,
And to meet the challenge on the way
    With a face shining bright with joy!

Rays of Hope...

From poems and promises
To ships and submarines;
From dreams that are left behind
To memories that linger in my mind,
I have seen this world, both far and near,
Lost and gained those who are true and dear.
Happy and precious moments faded like dew,
But their memories are always new;
Floating in my heart are days gone by,
Dancing like stars twinkling in dark blue sky.
They shed rays of hope, of peace, of promise,
Whisper softly, each day is Heavenly bliss;
Live and let live, and bury your sorrow,
Yet to come is a beautiful tomorrow!